DROP YOUR FISTS

AND

RAISE YOUR HANDS

DR DEBRA R WILSON

DEDICATED

In honor and memory of my mother,

Audrey Delores Epps-Wilson.

Her strength, endurance and love anchored me as

she watched me persevere to apply the principles,

Drop Your Fists and Raise Your Hands.

And

Kalah Renee and Autumn Corine, my daughters

who continue to be the wind beneath my wings.

TABLE OF CONTENTS

PREFACE

The Holy Spirit inspired me to write this book right in the middle of battle. I was a high-risk pregnancy with preeclampsia and gestational diabetes, my spouse was unemployed, I was asked to work beyond my pregnancy leave, and I was evicted while shouldering the financial weight for my family. I tried to hide my situation from my family, friends and those who continued to hate and criticize me amid my turmoil. It was in this season of dimension-climbing experiences that this book was born. *Dimension-climbing experiences* are the moments of anguish in our life that bring definition to our character and to our purpose. This is the best way to describe the dichotomy between understanding who *we* believe we are and discovering who *God* has called us to be; or, who *we* are trying to become while realizing it may not be quite what God intended.

I began to journal as a strategy to keep calm, keep emotionally connected and remain conscious to avoid resentment. At the same time, I fought hard to resist negative feelings, surroundings (people) or conversations that threatened my peace, my faith and my capacity to love.

We know that we have passed from death (dimension) to life (dimension), because we love each other. Anyone who does not love remains in death.

—*I John 3:14 (NIV)*

To love someone sincerely is to cross dimensions. To love someone who is difficult to love must be like crossing *several* dimensions.

I had to recognize that my experiences were "dimension-climbing" because every opposing force seemed to be working against me: shattered family relationships, abusive connections, false sense of relationships in the church, feeling taken advantage of, and the overwhelming financial struggles. In agreement, these maladies came against me to the degree that they launched me from one place to another emotionally, mentally, spiritually and at times physically. I felt torn, depressed, confused, felt that I was not enough; I forgot simple things and at times felt physically nauseous. I was literally going through the motions of living; dressed up on the outside with a smile, but inside I felt hollow and afraid. I lost trust in people, and at some point, I think I lost faith in myself. Somehow, however, I kept serving people, preaching, teaching, and encouraging.

God carried me through what would have destroyed me had I stayed *there* continuing to internally fight back or attempting to meander through it. If God had not rescued me from battles that I did not understand how to win, the experiences would have diminished my capacity to forgive and persevere. Basically, it would have taken me under.

Prior to beginning this writing project, I still believed that the ability to love was inherent and a part of human nature as opposed to something that needed to be cultivated, nurtured, and protected. While the love element seems to come naturally in the animal kingdom, humans struggle with loyalty, attention, sympathy, empathy, affection, and kindness. When love challenges us by the amount of work it involves or is destroyed by broken trust, shattered by abuse, or bruised by rejection, the resulting devastation can lead to life-altering consequences such as a broken home, addiction, promiscuity, regret, and thoughts of suicide for some.

For a season during this process, I came to the end of myself and cried out to God in emotional exhaustion. I heard God quietly, yet fervently say, *"Drop Your Fists and Raise Your Hands."* From that time and long after that breaking point, God would quietly remind me of this scripture.

...Be not afraid nor dismayed by reason of this great multitude; for the battle is not yours, but God's...

—2 Chronicles 20:15b (KJV)

Yes, I understood the verse, but I was taken aback when the great multitude of battle was in my core relationships: home, family, friends, and church family; especially those I thought were kind, saved, and sincere. Boy was I in shock! For some time, I felt disconnected. I was still coming into bloom within my own ministry and leadership development. It was like I had gone behind the curtain of "church," to what *really* happens behind the scenes and it hurt. It was hard to witness spiritual leaders bully young Christians with growing faith. It was difficult watching the manipulation and deliberate cruelty used to leverage emotional and mental control. This was not just one sect or one church, but this spirit was abroad Christendom. There was such callousness and falling away from the rudiment of true ministry-*love*. I think it is important for us to discuss this notion of bullying and manipulating further. When most people hear these terms, they tend to believe it does not describe their behavior. And, some people are so prone to being victims of this treatment that they do not realize their situation is dangerous and causing them to live with raised fists. When people come to others for sympathy, comfort, and healing, it is unfortunate when their vulnerabilities are taken advantage of. Instead of being given sincere love and understanding, they are accounted as a dumb sheep for an emotional slaughter. There are horror stories of people being talked about to the extent that they feel distant, disconnected, depressed, and suicidal because they trusted someone who was vile and deceptive. I have seen people excommunicated and ignored by leadership only because they made a typo on a program, or did not hit the right note during a song, or could not leave their family to attend a particular event. People who are young in their faith were made to feel guilt and shame for missing services, not giving money they did not have to give or refusing to do other inappropriate favors, sexual and otherwise. I have watched people who have positions that support the worship experience (musician, ministry staff, etc.) used for their gifts and talents, while their heart and soul remained damaged, undelivered and pushed by the wayside. Their contributions were more important than their life.

On some level, I felt trapped with no relief, no reprieve, and certainly no retreat because I was committed. I was vested and invested in people and my own leadership growth. I felt the strong sense of responsibility to protect innocent people from being hurt by vile dynamics. God did not let me just bail out of the situation, and I did not desire to. I refused to leave people stranded and alone. God wanted to groom me, to prepare me and to allow me to recognize the truth of my situation. I was in battle. And it seemed the more I defended others, the worse the battle became for me.

I have come to realize that it probably never will. *Dropping your fists and raising your hands* is a principle; therefore, it is a mode of conduct and a lifelong process. During this journey, I have changed, adjusted and then changed again so that my response to challenges, battles, or struggles is becoming filtered through a new lens. I am developing a new internal proclivity to *"drop my fists and raise my hands."*

This concept may sound like a cliché of, "Get over it," but it is much more than a simple, "Accept things for what they are and move on." This journey will challenge the heart, the mindset, our tucked away hurts, and the multi-layered reasons behind our raised fists by causing us to face our truth. The book will cause us to look into *our* mirrors without masks and away from the crowd. We will be able to search the deepest part of our hearts and see the what, who, how, when, and where our truth is to determine that it is now time to drop our fists and raise our hands.

This method is intended to provide a new strategy for overcoming obstacles, a new approach to handling the potholes in life before they become ditches or quicksand swamps. Those who take the journey will learn how to apply the manifold concepts that are discussed in this book. We will find out how to process situations before speaking prematurely, and we will also discover how to avoid drowning in a shallow pool that feels like an ocean.

Perception is an integral part of the principle, but praying is the most crucial part of the strategy. I discovered new attributes of God while writing this book. I have developed a relationship with God with full assurance that He is in me and that He is *for* me. As you take this journey, I am confident that you will make many new personal discoveries too.

I started the *Drop Your Fist and Raise Your Hands* project many years ago. At first, I believed that I was just writing to fulfill a lifelong passion to write a book. I can relate to those who write for release of stress, expression, or just to keep a record of life's events. The hurdles and roadblocks in my life have been surmountable, and each experience a definitive epilog. Through each circumstance, God enabled me to survive, overcome and triumph. As I started writing down my thoughts and feelings, I also began writing this book. It seemed that despite several failed attempts at completing this book over the past 16 years, I knew God was inspiring me and pushing me past my fears to finish it and to publish it to help others.

Drop Your Fist and Raise Your Hands is a response to the current cry of God's people, and as such, its healing message of surrender and deliverance will go out to the masses and not return to Him unaccomplished.

INTRODUCTION

Drop Your Fists and Raise Your Hands is a concept that can become a way of life. As we discuss and discover examples of people who have successfully applied this methodology to everyday challenges, we will begin to understand the relevance and timeliness of this fundamental principle.

The Bible story about Joseph is an excellent place to begin this journey because it illustrates the theoretical framework for *Drop Your Fists and Raise Your Hands*. The theoretical framework is the structure that can back up or support a theory. Joseph, perhaps a familiar story to some, was a man in the Bible, who was the younger, said to be, overconfident son of Jacob. Joseph had the gifts of dreams and interpreting the dreams of others. He was seen as his father's favorite and for this cause his ten older brothers sold him to slave traders and told their father he was dead. Joseph would hurdle over constant life battles such as imprisonment, false accusation, deception, betrayal, but would then overcome these hurdles and live a life of favor, triumph, prosperity and restoration.

We will discover what makes the principle of *Drop Your Fists and Raise Your Hands* relevant and refer to the *Spiritual Framework of Coping* as our support.

Like Joseph and his older brothers, we will see how God is able to turn the enemy's agenda for our destruction into an overwhelming blessing. We will also come to realize that this will not happen without a process. God's blessing is so much more than just material gain because God's divine and supernatural blessings are life-changing. It was not just Joseph who learned lessons in humility, courage, and responsible empowerment; his father, his brothers, and an entire nation felt the impact of these experiences.

We tend to focus on Joseph in the story because he seems to be the main character and most people like to associate their life with a story's hero. In this story; however, Joseph's brothers are practical examples of individuals in modern society. Even though the story goes back thousands of years, many people we live among and interact with display the same unrighteous behavior that was illustrated by Joseph's brothers.

Jealousy and cruelty are not just emotions exemplified or amplified by unchurched people or terrorists. These feelings and the actions that are propelled by them are not associated with the evilest people in our society; ordinary folks can fall prey to these emotions as well.

For Joseph to actualize his purpose, he had to stop being the victim. He had to learn the concept of *dropping your fists and raising your hands* in the midst of rejection, disconnection, abuse, imprisonment and abandonment. His brothers hated him because:

a) he was favored by his father
b) he was gifted by God
c) he testified of his anticipation
d) his favor threatened their self-worth

Have you ever been hated by someone based upon their perception of you alone? They hate you because they feel that something about you may threaten *their* self-worth. Just like Joseph, we may find some unpleasant bridges to cross as we heal beyond our hurting places and progress into our life's purpose.

Let's take a moment to think about this in an exercise.

EXERCISE # 1
PERCEPTION POISON

This exercise explores "perception poison." Perception Poison is the notion that another person's *negative* perception of us can *poison* our self-perception and have an adverse impact on our thought process and our behavior. Negative perceptions can be criticisms that seem intended to cause hurt, bring shame, embarrass, diminish and intimidate another person.

People often allow the perceptions, opinions, and expectations of others to influence their self-efficacy.

In the story of Joseph, he did not seem to allow his brother's perception to change his mind, lessen his confidence or threaten his convictions.

This exercise makes it possible to ponder how we respond to negative perceptions. The questions below encourage us to think about instances in life when we felt that someone attempted to lessen our confidence by their negative perceptions or opinions.

You can write your answers here or in the 21 Day Reflection Journal. It is important to ponder if your experiences have caused raised fists. It is necessary to work through the questions below in order to begin the process of *dropping your fists and raising your hands*.

1) Have you ever experienced someone's attempt to poison your self-perception?
   a) Who was the person?
   b) What was their role or relationship to you?
   c) Do you remember how the experience felt?

2) From your perspective was this experience fueled by jealousy, resentment or some other motivation?
   a) Is this experience ongoing or just a *tabloid drive by*? A *tabloid drive by* is when an individual makes an assumption without any information about you.

3) What was your response?
   a) How did you overcome?

4) Have you ever been accused of trying to poison someone's self-esteem?

5) Was the accusation true?
   a) If so, what caused you to behave this way? Jealousy? Insecurity? Anger?

b) If not, why do you believe they felt this way?

c) If there was an opportunity to discuss the issue, what was the outcome?

This exercise shows us that we can experience poison perception as a victim or as an accused offender.

What do we do now that we answered the questions?

We should take this opportunity to search within to see if we harbor any negative feelings from being a victim of poison perceptions.

- Do we need to forgive someone in our hearts for their attempt to hurt us?
- Do we need to stand strong and refuse to allow another person's perception to influence our self-esteem, self-efficacy, and choices?
- Do we need to be mindful of how our interactions with others could be perceived as poison to their self-esteem?

This is a good place to journal your feelings in the Drop Your Fists and Raise Your Hands 21 Days of Reflection Journal.

This exercise challenged us to ponder and search our hearts for any unresolved feelings that may cause us to have raise fists. As we journal our responses and feelings, we can decide to make the choice to surrender our *negative* feelings. Surrendering our feelings means letting them go.

Remember, Acknowledge, Drop, and Raise (R.A.D.A.R.)!

Perhaps answering some of those questions dredged up some painful memories. These type of experiences feel like emotional drive-by's, where someone just runs you over emotionally and leaves you wounded, ready to hit you again or willing to let you just bleed out and die. Sometimes, these emotional hits happen by people who do not even know you, understand you and have not taken the time to really know your story, your struggles, your failures, your fears, etc. And contrary to popular sexist belief, women are not the only ones who exhibit this type of catty behavior; men have issues of hateration, too.

We learn a valuable lesson from the story of Joseph and his brothers.

- We have to be careful who we share our dreams and aspirations with. I believe we have to share it by faith to set it in motion, for it to come to life, but we have to know the audience we share with.
- Everybody will not share in the celebration of your successes. People closest to you may not be able to handle God's blessings upon your life.

Joseph was the object of a hate so vehement that his very being, as perceived by his brothers, was a threat to *their* being. The Bible reminds us that jealousy is as cruel as the grave; meaning that sometimes, jealous people kill the person they are envious of because of some crazy notion that taking them out will somehow remove the threat and salvage *their* shortcomings. If these people make it to prison to mull over how irrational their motivation was, they might eventually realize that someone else's success should actually *inspire* positive change and not corruption. The worst reality of this madness is that there are people in our circle of life that would rather see us dead than to witness our success.

Joseph's dream revealed that he would eventually become both leader and lender to his older brothers, but the dream was not the only source of contention. The father favored Joseph and openly set him apart from his brothers, covering him with an elaborate coat of many colors.

Let's discuss favor for a moment. Has God ever publicly blessed you and provided you with His favor to the degree that you felt put on blast? Oh, you accepted the blessing, praised God for the favor, and humbly recognized the grace and mercy, but you may not have realized the precarious position you would be in among those around you. Ironically, our blessings often come with harsh lessons regarding loyalty and friendships.

Sometimes, the person who appears to be the biggest supporter of your success might secretly be your worst enemy. They appreciate what your blessing does for them, but hate you for being the one chosen to *carry* the blessing.

They love you, and then they grow to hate the very thing that caused them to love you in the first place. Wow! Sounds crazy? It is! And you can almost sit back with a bucket of popcorn and a soft drink watching them go through *their* personal drama because of *your* blessing and their perception of how it impacts *them*. Of course, amid all of this, they are missing the way to their *own* blessings.

Let's spend some time in the mind of the *Hater*. The term Hater describes a person who *cannot* be happy for another's success, achievement, lifestyle, or freedom; and as a result, they make an effort to point out perceived flaws, weaknesses, and vulnerabilities of that person. The Hater is not necessarily fueled by jealousy or wanting to replace the person they criticize, they just want the person to be less of a success, or perhaps, to feel less free, or just to be taken down. Why?

I am sure there are a myriad of explanations people give for being over critical of a person they should be happy for and celebrate with. Perhaps the hater feels inferior, limited, intimidated, or just fails to realize that God's blessings are open to them if they would have faith and believe. People can actually be a hater to those they claim to love, but due to an unresolved issue deep within, they cannot be happy for that person. This dynamic happens among family, friends, co-workers, students, church members, etc. Sometimes people do not even realize that they are being haters because their tendency to find fault with someone has become their typical response. Hateration spawns from an unfulfilled heart; from feeling that one did not receive an opportunity, a fair chance, appropriate resources or provision. As a result, fists are raised, and people become critical of others, negative, condescending, sarcastic, and just plain ol' *mean*. Everyone is susceptible to being a *hater*. We have to search our heart to find the root of these feelings and then make a choice to confront it.

This brings us to another story that illustrates the concept of *Drop Your Fists and Raise Your Hands*: The Biblical story of Cain and Abel, the two sons of Adam and Eve. Cain was a farmer who grew vegetables and grains while Abel was a shepherd who took care of the family's cattle. The boys were instructed to prepare an offering to God to show their appreciation for His bountiful blessings of living in the beautiful Garden of Eden. Abel, the shepherd, took the time to find the most precious lamb of great value and worth to offer God. He gave up a lamb without blemishes, the most expensive one in the herd. Cain, the gardener, gave *straw*, which was not of *any* value or sacrifice to what he possessed. Cain simply could not understand why God needed an offering and figured that his raggedy straw was good enough to throw back at God.

God responded to both sacrifices; He completely received Able's offering but somewhat rejected Cain's offering. God preferred Abel's offering over Cain's based on the *intention* behind their giving. For this reason, Cain developed hate in his heart toward Abel. We ask ourselves, how could Cain be angry with Abel? This is the plight of the *hater:* failure to recognize cause and effect, refusal to accept responsibility and being too prideful to change. God went so far as to have a personal conversation with Cain to reason with him and to let him know how he could be equally blessed if he would humble his heart and change his mind.

What an opportunity it is for God to extend His mercy and His grace to help us out of our own mess—face to face even. Unfortunately, instead of Cain listening to God and accepting the fact that he had to change his mind and his heart to obtain a blessing, he chose to hate and then *kill* his brother. Cain killed his brother Abel with foolish pride, callous jealousy, and hatred in his heart. The spirit of Cain rests upon us today. This type of relentless anger is the cause of many calamities in our society; murder, slander, drug pushing, adultery, abuse, etc.

What do we take away from Able's legacy? Perhaps we learn how much our heart and mindset affects our willingness to drop our fists and raise our hands. The concept of drop your fists and raise your hands fosters peace; peace within ourselves and peace with God. It is a concept that affects every area of our life. Abel teaches us how to please God by giving with a sincere heart. Abel pleased God. That is his legacy. What we purpose in our heart is important to God. How many people actually please God today? Is that even their focus anymore?

Blessings and Bosting

Let's look at Joseph's life a little more. Have you ever been blessed to the degree that you became boastful? After Joseph was adorned with the coat of many colors by his father, he may have used every opportunity to rub the coat in his brother's face. In my imagination, I see Joseph wearing the coat and prancing around where the brothers were hard at work since he was the youngest and free to play. He probably showed up to every meal in the coat. He may have even worn the coat to play and perhaps made a production while taking it off, folding it just so and making sure he was seen in full effect. And when he revealed the dream God gave him concerning his purpose, which included reigning over his brothers, he may have told it at the dinner table, even causing his father to raise an eyebrow.

In Joseph's dream, he and his brothers were working in a field when suddenly his sheaf of the grain rose and stood upright while his brothers' sheaves gathered around to his and bowed down to it. If that was not enough, Joseph had another dream that the sun and the moon and eleven stars bowed down to him. Even Joseph's father had issues with his dreams, asking him if he was insinuating that his whole family would one day come and bow down to the ground before him. The brothers became jealous and hated Joseph while the father quietly pondered his dreams.

When foolish or immature people are granted favor, it can sometimes lead to their detriment. Not that Joseph was evil or arrogant, but perhaps a bit foolish in the way he shared the information. Because he was just a child, he did not understand how the dream would be perceived or received by his family.

So the coat, Joseph's behavior, the father's favor, and then the revelation of his dream was just too much for his brothers to take. If Joseph's dream materialized, it would mean that he, the spoiled brat with the colorful coat, would be their ruler. His behavior was not worthy of such hate and certainly did not warrant being sold or left for dead, but his brothers were operating under the same self-serving sense of entitlement as Cain.

I am learning that when people fear, it can sometimes breed contempt. People fear what they do not understand. People often fear what could be a blessing to them if they just took the time to wait, watch, ask questions, and resist the temptation to ridicule.

The people slander whatever they do not understand, and the very things they do understand by instinct—as irrational animals do—will destroy them.

Woe unto them! They have taken the way of Cain.

—Jude 1:10-11a (NIV)

Joseph's brothers were emotionally distraught after they sold him, and there was much conflict among them after they committed the crime. To make matters worse, they had to watch their father suffer after they lied to him about Joseph's disappearance. Joseph's father was left in anguish without a true explanation. Fear and misunderstanding can transform into anger that broods and boils over until an individual commits a heinous act that affects everyone around them. The people affected by such crimes are often left without explanation, just like Joseph's father. The devastation can be so heavy that those affected may never heal.

Like Joseph and Abel, Kind David was another biblical character who experienced wrongdoing at the hands of family members. When David was brought into a dinner that his father excluded him from with the Prophet Samuel and his older brothers, God anointed him as the next King. What do we take away from *this* story? How might David have felt, knowing that he was not even invited to dinner with his family and their special guest? Imagine coming into the house, dinner is smelling good, and everybody is dressed in their Sunday-best, and there you are, uninvited, *and* unwelcome. Your family doesn't want you there, but they allow you to stay because their *guest* insists. You are not dressed, dirty in fact, with no opportunity to acclimate to the setting before you. You do realize; however, that you were left out, rejected, and not considered worthy, but you are not even given time to process it because before you can even blink, God pours out a blessing upon you and anoints you right in the middle of what looks like a mess. I believe this is why David later wrote in Psalm 23:5:

"You prepare a table before me in the presence of my enemies. You anoint my head with oil; my cup overflows."

When Prophet Samuel anointed David as King of Israel in front of his father and brothers, the Bible says that he went back to the field he was called from and continued to shepherd the sheep until the appointed time. Wow! How many people are willing to do this today? He *dropped his fists and raised his hands*. However, the rejection and the suppressed pain of being the "black sheep" of the family would later manifest into other habits, bad choices and detrimental consequences for David and the generations that followed. David committed adultery with his soldier's wife, got her pregnant and then arranged for the soldier's death. David was so busy running around sinning that he didn't realize his children were out committing, in some cases, even more atrocious acts. One of them committed rape and incest, (which led to another son killing him.) Another son, Absalom, would revolt against him and lead a rebellion to take over his throne, which only led to his own demise. David would become stubborn and ignore advice resulting in a deadly plague affecting everyone he was responsible for. David suffered great loss. But, in spite of these obstacles, David's life exemplified the principle of *drop your fists and raise your hands*, and he was considered "a man after God's own heart" simply because David was a Worshipper. He knew how to humble himself, come to God broken after he failed, ask God to cleanse him, restore him, and then try again to please God. David would spend his lifetime applying this principle. He endured struggles, experienced heartache, battled in his home, waged wars against nations, lost moral challenges and suffered consequences. But David would always find his way back in God's presence with R.A.D.A.R.; recognizing his issues, addressing his situation, dropping his fists *and* raising his hands.

Drop your fists and raise your hands is not intended for the perfect, but for the flawed, the failed, the diseased and the discontented, who, in spite of these human frailties, contend to apply the principle. By applying this principle, we have hope and we are able to persevere and to reap bountiful blessings despite our situations. We can overcome, heal, start over, seize new opportunities, and experience abundant living with joy and in peace.

COMMERCIAL BREAK

Have we learned how to ponder? This is a process worth putting into practice. To ponder is to take the time to *think things through*. I am learning to reject my tendency to just jump at what I believe I hear God saying to me or what He is trying to show me without processing what I heard. I used to hear God *begin* to speak something into me, through a dream, or a revelation, or by experiencing an "Aha moment;" but before God could give me the intent or the meaning, I would run with it and begin making plans. Really? Sometimes we need to have a seat until we are asked to do otherwise. Every encounter is not an invitation.

But Mary kept all these things, and pondered them in her heart.

—*Luke 2:19*

The excitement of new information or an encounter with truth can sometimes make it difficult to keep still, but it is necessary to avoid the leap. Like Mary, the mother of Jesus, we need to learn how to keep all things and to ponder them in our heart. Regardless of how exciting the revelation or the "Aha moment," is, it is necessary to relax, to hold on, to breathe, and to ponder.

I am learning how to ponder long enough for God to actually finish His sentence and how to make my way safe before I jump into action. This saves me time and embarrassment. I do not want to waste time missing divine opportunities simply because I did not take the time to ponder.

Back to the story of David...

David kept his anointing to himself, pondered the encounter in his heart, and went back to what he was doing until time and opportunity dictated something new. Was David resented by his older brothers? I am sure that he was. That particular scene prompted God to challenge the Prophet because even Prophet Samuel was confused. He did not know who to anoint, so he made assumptions, looking on the outward appearance of Jesse's sons to determine who would be the next King. God chastised Samuel to let him know that he was judging the situation based upon a person's outward countenance, while God makes choices based on a person's heart. These events also put David's father on notice and caused the jaws of his brothers to drop. The black sheep of the family, the rejected stone which the builders rejected, had now become the chief among them.

God has a blessing upon your life that will drop the jaws of those who feel more qualified or more worthy. *Ponder these things.*

Similar to David's story, God also put Joseph's father on notice. Although Joseph's father was proud of him, he caused discord in the home by openly preferring Joseph over his other sons. Did Joseph's father dote on his other boys the way he did Joseph? It does not sound like it.

Many of us can relate to either side of this story. Perhaps we were favored when we least expected it. Sometimes we are favored simply because those intended for the blessing forfeited. On the other hand, when people do not feel favored, they may perhaps feel rejected. Parents, if they are not careful, can cause great division in their home by favoring one child over the other children. Every child is unique with tailored needs. We cannot write the script of our children's lives, but we can certainly set them up for success by providing a safe, loving home environment where they can freely express themselves. Leaders, if not careful and fair, can cause great discord within their organization by not providing appropriate and equal opportunities among their employees.

Every person has unique talents and abilities. A good parent, just like an effective leader, provides a fair balance by nurturing their children's talents and helping them strengthen their deficiencies. If these balances do not occur, we may raise children who go through life with raised fists in every situation.

Fairness in leadership helps to prevent unnecessary conflict. We learn the term "fair" early in life, especially once we begin the process of socialization. We begin to define fair based upon life experiences. This frames our perception and impacts our relationships. Our perception of what is fair can also cause us to raise our fists in situations instead of allowing God to make things right on our behalf. Once established, our concept of what is fair is deep-seated and only altered by what we continue to experience in life and perhaps by situations that take us through broken places. Both Joseph and his brothers defined and then redefined fairness based upon the issues they faced in life. This can be the place of great transformation and where we may learn that there comes a point in our lives when we have to "drop our fists and raise our hands."

HOW TO USE THIS BOOK

Drop Your Fists and Raise Your Hands is an interactive book designed to be a collaborative experience. Together, we will discover what causes raised fists, learn the purpose and the process of dropping them, and then learn how to raise our hands. Serious life-changing concepts are interspersed with humor as I write directly from my heart to yours.

I purposely made this book easy-to-read. The concepts are relatable, retainable, and readily applicable. There will be segments of *Commercial Breaks* where God *"stopped the press"* to drop in a Word of Knowledge.

There will be *Reflections* where I share my personal application of the lessons learned while on this journey.

Meaningful Moments are where I share snippets of real life events that will showcase this principle in action and hopefully make this journey real and tangible for you.

I encourage you to become an active *participant* by completing the exercises. The exercises are strategically placed throughout the book so that you can write about your experiences as they relate to the book's principles. It is my hope that these exercises will allow you to express yourself while also challenging your thinking and enlightening your heart.

I encourage you to allow time for reflection and to perhaps journal your feelings and thoughts as you read the book. Again, for you to become an *active* participant in this journey, I strongly suggest reading this book sequentially; the personal inserts are shared respectively to keep the information in context and to ensure that you fully receive the intended message in each section. You will gain more insight and experience change if you walk through this process step-by-step with me. Skipping sections (or reading out of order) may cause you to miss messages that are designed to facilitate healing, closure, and in some cases, a fresh outlook and new beginning.

The two-part principle was divinely given to me during a season of anguish and despair, but I knew that to fully develop this theory, I needed to do a bit of research. I searched for a theoretical framework that would support the fundamental concepts of my theory: coping with unresolved issues by deep introspection and surrendering to God as our source of help, healing, and strength. I used my personal experiences, along with selected methodologies from The Spiritual Framework of Coping, to fully develop this process.

I believe this book will be helpful for those in all walks of faith, from the novice to the veteran, and I am overjoyed that you have decided to take this journey with me.

THE SPIRITUAL
FRAMEWORK OF COPING

This book is balanced with spiritual and natural truths, events of my life's experiences and examples from my life's struggles and triumphs. The premise of this work is for us to understand the nature and the role of how each realm,— spiritual and natural, influences our ability to cope with the stress of holding on to past hurts, to adapt to a new way of processing emotional challenges, to become flexible in our response to obstacles and to heal beyond "here." Helping you to achieve Holistic Health is the ultimate goal of *Drop Your Fists and Raise Your Hands.*

The Spiritual Framework of Coping came from a Scholarly Article as a result of many years of research to associate the influence of religion and/or spirituality on stress, coping, and health. Most of the research concerning this effort was conducted by K.I.Pargament, beginning in 1997, using a transactional model of stress and coping. Kenneth I. Pargament is licensed in Clinical Psychology and an emeritus professor of psychology. He has published over 200 articles on the subject of religion and spirituality in psychology and studies various relationships between religion, psychological well-being and stress, as well as other closely related subjects. In 1997, his research focused on the process of religious coping with emphasis on three key components: *Spiritual appraisals*, *Person Factors*, and *Meaning-Making*.

Spiritual Appraisals

Spiritual appraisals is a concept used to describe how people process coping with stress, illness, accidents and other negative life events. It is the notion that people use spiritual causal attributions as a common way to understand these occurrences. The concept indicates that attributions to God may help people preserve their belief in a just world, which in turn helps them hold on to a sense of personal control when confronted with uncontrollable situations. The process of appraisal represents an individual's view of specific spiritual coping methods that could be used in response to a stressor. In other words, it is the process that people go through as they look to God for help in dealing with issues that they feel hopeless in trying to change for themselves.

Person Factors

Person factors involve how a person's religious denomination and doctrinal beliefs direct how they will cope with life stressors. It is found that religious-oriented lifestyles tend to be healthier with reduced occurrences of disease. Further, it is believed that people who have internalized a deep belief system in their faith rely on their religious resources in times of crisis, especially if the event is perceived to be out of their personal control. This is referred to as *intrinsic religion*, where a person chooses to believe without an external motive. Simply, by faith. Researchers found that intrinsic religious orientation provided individuals with a sense of meaning when dealing with severe stress and resulted in a successful healing process as well as a predictive decline in depression. Researchers refer to intrinsic religion as being more mature because it is personally chosen as opposed to extrinsic religion which is motivated by external factors such as social acceptance and advancement. Pargament indicated that studies indicate religious coping styles affected the levels of anxiety experienced in a group of cardiac transplant candidates. It is believed that a collaborative relationship with God appears to provide individuals with a sense of empowerment in the face of difficult situations. Other studies implicate that a belief in God's control is a factor in coping with health-related issues.

A 1998 study of coronary bypass surgery found that over 50% of patients who chose private prayer as the most frequent practice out of a list of 21 non-medical help-seeking or coping behaviors experienced less discomfort post-surgery. In 1999, a study of caregivers concluded that prayer might be the most profound religious coping behavior. In fact, this study proposed that an individual experiences a sense of "shared" control with God that includes their own sense of responsibility in coping with stress.

More recent studies in 2000 proposed that a surrendering style of spiritual problem-solving involves an active decision to release personal control to God over those aspects of life that fall outside of one's control. This is believed to provide an emotionally overwhelmed individual some relief and a sense of assurance that God is in charge of the situation. Breast cancer survivors, for example, reported feeling a sense of relief by sharing their burden with God (Gall & Cornbalt, 2002). These types of results have led researchers to conclude that a just and benevolent God provides individuals with a *framework* of control that is perceived as more trustworthy than leaving things up to chance.

Based upon research, people who used spiritual coping reported the following benefits:

- A positive impact on the healing process
- Lower depression, greater happiness, and greater life satisfaction
- Better self-health
- Lower alcohol consumption in patients
- Fewer somatic complaints
- Increased social activity
- Fewer interpersonal problems
- Lower mortality

These are just a few examples of how Person Factors can positively impact coping and healing. Another component of religious coping, *Meaning-Making*, explains how spirituality can influence one's perception of stressful life events.

Meaning Making

Pargament (1997) found that religion and/or spirituality play an important role in finding *meaning* in a stressful event. In fact, situational meaning involves an individual making an event less threatening by actually seeing opportunities for growth in the situation. Meaning-making involves a change in perspective because of one's faith. Further, meaning-making results in the reframing of a stressful event as a spiritual *opportunity* that offers benefits and change to gain insights about life. Research reports that life-threatening events may serve as "wake-up" calls to take stock of life and rearrange priorities *based upon* one's spirituality. On the other hand, it is reported that stressful events can also be interpreted as punishment for something bad. They can also be perceived as a test, a form of purification, or a challenge meant to be mastered. In the latter, individuals are apt to believe that God would not give them more than they could handle.

Another study reported that reframing and the influence of spirituality on meaning-making is the possibility of seeing oneself as having a limited ability to understand the entirety of events and becoming content with not finding a "reason" for suffering, pain, etc. (Pargament, 1992)

More recently, a 2002 study found that spirituality can help people center an event within the context of a "bigger picture," or master plan. Once an individual uses spirituality to perceive a deeper purpose, troubling circumstances take on new meaning and can be seen as something that was *meant* to happen as opposed to something that occurred randomly.

Current work on meaning-making and spirituality is focused on a process researchers term "sanctification": applying spiritual character and significance to secular aspects of life. Researchers report that with sanctification, an event can be experienced as a manifestation of God *based upon* one's belief, image of or experiences with God.

The Spiritual Framework of Coping, along with Biblical truths and real-life events, provide theoretical, spiritual, and practical learning tools for confronting issues that cause emotional turmoil. The framework substantiates that life events and negative perception of those events, can cause raised fists; however, spirituality and personal choice can allow us to simply *raise our hands*.

By using the concepts and exercises provided in *Drop Your Fists and Raise Your Hands*, you will actively work towards developing a new personal arsenal of emotional, spiritual and practical strength. You will also work through past pain to get closure, facilitate change, and empower yourself to make positive life choices every day.

Change will not come if we wait for some other person or some other time. We are the ones we've been waiting for. We are the change that we seek–

— Barack Obama

CHAPTER BREAK

CHAPTER 1
THE BATTLE CONTINUES

What has been will be again, what has been done will be done again; there is nothing new under the sun.

—Ecclesiastes 1:9 (NIV)

The challenges, obstacles, frustrations, and hurts of today can make life seem like a constant war-zone. Why do we face such strife? This is a perfect place to open the discussion, but first, I have some important and timely information about the battle we all face—*it is not new.*

The battle could mean many different things: the battle in our mind, our heart, our soul. We face a battle at every turn. What we are challenged with, opposed by, and struggling to overcome is *real*. It may catch us off guard, threaten to cause anguish, disguise itself as a blessing to dismantle us, and will no doubt serve to distract, but it is not a *new* battle.

We are using the singular noun "battle" because the term indicates a *large* scale and a long

33

duration of time that encompasses multiple elements, categories, dimensions, etc. It is one *battle* with many facets, implications, weapons, fights, and zones. It is indicative of what challenges us in this life.

We may be facing something life-changing or feel like we are in the middle of a war, but the advantage of knowing that the battle is not new provides an opportunity for a changed perspective and perhaps a different response.

The goal of *drop your fists and raise your hands* is not just sustainability in battle, but the goal is to provide a strategy for continual victory in and out of battle. If there was ever a time that we needed a fresh perspective and a well thought out strategy, that time is right now. With the current climate in our society, the time for dealing with the battle in a deliberate way is now. *Drop your fists and raise your hands* is a concept that offers a new approach to the way we respond to a battle.

Some of the most popular books and movies surround the theme of triumph in spite of adversity. For those of us who like action type books and films, we are intrigued by the suspense of the struggle, the fight, the variable scenes and the victory of the main character. In the most gripping movies that hint at a sequel, there has to be evidence alluding to an unfinished battle (or the emergence of a new one). It is the anticipation that captures our attention. When the sequel of a good movie arrives, we become eager to learn how the battle will pick up where it left off in the previous movie. We mentally and sometimes emotionally replay the scenes from the first movie in our head to prepare ourselves for the sequel. While drama or suspense may be entertaining to watch, it is not fun to experience in real life.

Our life is an action movie, but if it becomes smothered in drama and suspense, it can feel like we are suffocating. Know this; we are *not* alone in our experiences. We all will suffer loss at some point in our lives; loss of a person we cherish, perhaps the loss of a relationship, employment, an opportunity or our possessions. We all will experience hurt, brokenness, failure, a set-back, and disappointment. The battle we encounter is not uncommon, but rather a continuing sequel of life, a sequel that originates from recorded Biblical events as well as our practical life experiences.

I have a jewel of wisdom for you, but unlike a movie cliffhanger, I won't leave you in suspense: we are in a *continuous* battle. After reading this book and implementing the strategies presented, my hope is that you will learn to intrinsically *drop your fists and raise your hands* in response to adversity.

There are two realms where we will encounter warfare: the spiritual realm and the natural. These encounters are not new to anyone, particularly to people who are of Christian faith. The war in these realms is inherent to life, especially once we are born-again believers because we begin to understand the dimensions of battle. This is not solely a Christian concept, however. In life, there will be opposition and conflict. This is true for all humankind. We are born in conflict. Our struggle in the labor process is just the beginning of a lifelong battle. What is the battle over? The spoil.

Spoil refers to goods, worth, and valuables. Goods that are so important, people will wage war to get them. In fact, spoil, or perceived spoil, has been the cause of many wars over centuries in many countries, communities, in politics, and even in families. Where there is no spoil, there is no need for battle. A battle occurs when there is something worth fighting for. *We* are the spoil to every battle in our life. Why? God and the enemy are fighting for our surrender as we are of such great value. We are valuable because we have a divine purpose and even more so because God loves us. We are *worth* the opposition between God and the enemy. We are *worth* the conflict. God deemed us worthy to die for so *surely* we are worth fighting for. Moreover, because of our great worth to God, we are of great spoil to the enemy. Therefore, our attempt to avoid opposition will not prohibit this uninvited and certainly unwelcomed guest from intruding in our lives. The battle we encounter is sometimes short-lived, and at times, it appears that it never ceases.

The battle we face today is, in essence, a sequel to what has been happening over centuries, even before the birth, death, and resurrection of Jesus

Christ. This does not dismiss our struggles, challenges, frustrations, and casualties that may occur in the battle because they are *real*. The blessed assurance we have is that the battle is divinely fixed in our favor to win! Although the battle is intended for our victorious outcome, we still have to live through it.

The first level of battle introduced to man is the one we face on the inside of us, the battle to be *free*. How can freedom be a battle when the word freedom, by definition, denotes a lack of restriction or resistance? *Freedom* is a battle because there is resistance going on inside of us. Our free will provides autonomy to choose what is right when there is adversity within us tempting us to do what is wrong.

Let us review an illustration about this freedom of will by reviewing the events in the lives of the first people God created, Adam and Eve. God placed Adam and Eve in the Garden of Eden with dominion over all things living but required they should not eat of a particular tree in the garden. God created them with a free will and gave them instruction, but He did *not* take away their freedom to choose. Well, we are familiar with the choice Adam and Eve made with their free will—to eat of that very tree God told them not to.

Does God stop *us* from choosing to engage in battles that we are not prepared for? Of course, He *attempts* to stop us by sending people, circumstances, and places in our way to deter us, provide a warning, expose danger, or give us a way of escape to make it almost impossible to proceed. But, do we stop? Do we listen? Do we at least proceed with caution? Hmmm. Some people have it in their minds that if God does not *stop* us, He is co-signing on our decisions or giving us a "high-five" for an obviously bad choice. It is amazing how we can hear God *clearly* when He sends messages that we *want* to hear, but we need confirmation and a prayer revival when He challenges our choices or allows us to go through something that is uncomfortable.

A battle builds character and should encourage better judgment. When we choose to engage in battles not intended for us to fight, we go against God's intent for us and sometimes, He allows us to work it out and come to *end of ourselves*. We come to this point when we hit a place that we cannot fix, gloss over, find a solution for, or recover from. During this time, most will surrender and drop their fists and raise their hands. For example, an insubordinate employee who has repeatedly been warned about their behavior may come to the *end of themselves* when they are terminated and escorted away from their job. The college student may come to the place where they drop their fists when they are dropped from school for academic failure because they spend more time going to parties than focusing on school. The abused spouse may come to this place when they are laying up in the hospital disfigured. Likewise, the abusing spouse may arrive at this place when they are sitting in a jail cell with time to process their actions. God will sometimes allow us to grow from bad judgment until we come back around to where we left *Him*. Gaining better judgment is one of the best outcomes of a battle because it helps us learn how to enter the ring to win the next time or how to stay out of the ring we were never invited in to. God allows us to encounter battle to wean us from immaturity and to make us grow by changing our perceptions and perspectives.

Adam and Eve not only experienced a pitfall in their judgment, but they encountered shame and suffered grave consequences. We are still living out the consequences of their free will. Since the fall of Adam and Eve, we have to work to eat, live, and survive. This poses a sobering question; what decisions are we making with our freedom that could affect the generations after us? We can ask ourselves this question personally, in our communities, and as a nation.

Just something to ponder.

COMMERCIAL BREAK

"Why are you fighting the air?" This is the question God asked me when I was shadowboxing while learning how to deal with a situation He wanted me to face. I did not understand His question initially because I was confident that I was doing all the right "things" to address the issue. In actuality, I was just beating the air.

I was praying, fasting, and studying every scripture about my issues, etc., but never dealing with the person or the situation. People at work would attempt to *throw me under the bus* by blaming me for an outcome I was not responsible for and then show up in my office later like nothing happened. I would get *side-swiped* by church folk who would talk about me behind my back and then ask me to pray for them like I did not have discernment. By never actually confronting the people or the problem, I was just shadowboxing. In time, I realized all I was essentially doing was having a wonderful private devotion but still avoiding the battle.

We can get caught up in the methodology of a spiritual script, but if we don't apply the methods, we will never resolve anything. If we never confront our issues, we are just beating the air. Or worse, sticking our heads in the sand. We are often taught sarcastic responses to lessen the impact that a painful experience may have on our life. Sometimes, God is in fact, allowing the challenge on purpose and for purpose.

Sarcastic responses are another form of shadowboxing. Phrases like, "It is what it is," or "Oh well," intimate a lack of willingness or desire to *challenge* our situations. I had to learn how to fight right.

Every time someone would attempt to provoke me with tales from the crypt (gossip, drama, mess, etc.), I would get my feelings hurt but would rarely respond to avoid conflict and to keep the peace. I would rehearse my response to myself over and over, but still avoid the necessary confrontation. Shadowboxing. It became a vicious cycle that left me with raised emotional fists. I would complain while not dealing with the issue straight on because I was trying to spare my offender's feelings at the expense of my own. My first encounter with this cycle began early in life when I arbitrarily became my mother's bodyguard against my father. I reserved my opinion and disdain of my dad's abuse out of respect, fear, and cultural mores; children did *not* get into grown-folks' business. I became torn between what was expected of me and what I felt compelled to do—protect and defend my mother.

Other encounters would come as I matriculated through college, entered the corporate world, became licensed in ministry and survived my own abusive relationships. As I was transitioning from a local community college to a University, I sat with my counselor who lived on my block. He questioned my high English scores in amazement as he *assumed* that I was from a "black community." This was my first *feeling* of racism. Although my feelings were hurt, I told the counselor that I lived on *his* block and that I attend school with his son. He was shocked. Hmmmmm. I was the youngest manager in most companies when I started working in my field of study, and executives would often make the mistake of assuming I could not participate in conversations at their level. Imagine their amazement when I started facilitating *their* meetings. Or, when clients would call to make an appointment with the manager and show up to find that *I* was the person they spoke to on the phone, and, in most cases, I was the manager they would be meeting with. Even in the church arena, I have been asked to operate in roles that woman typically do not operate in, like Administrative Assistant (Overseer), Department President, Executive Assistant, etc. This causes a level of discomfort for some, but the added value of my service shuts up the critics. Other people's attempts to diminish my presence by abuse, rejection, or abandonment has hurt, but *never* stopped my progress. God taught me how to respond and not to over react or make unwarranted adjustments.

I therefore so run, not as uncertainly; so I fight, not as one that beateth the air: But I keep under my body and bring it into subjection: lest that by any means, when I have preached to others, I myself should be a castaway.

—*I Corinthians 9:26-27 (KJV)*

I am learning to live beyond my feelings while confronting error and accepting the truth—the truth in me, about me, and even though sometimes begrudgingly, the truth in others. Through much travail, I have grown to be one to 'call it like it is.' I am consistent with this approach in the mirror and also with my children, my business, my ministry, and to those in authority. As a result, God has blessed me with opportunities to grow into a leader both spiritually and in the corporate arena. I have had the privilege of leading my mother to the Lord, fostering an intervention to help my brother fight drug addiction, and witnessing my father "take care of his soul business," as he expressed before he passed.

I stopped shadowboxing long ago, and I am not one to beat the air anymore. After what I have endured, if the enemy is crazy enough to bring it, I will sho-nuf finish it!

God created us with a free will, and just like Adam and Eve, we are free moral agents. Paul reminds us that we are born with an internal battle in Romans, chapter 7. Can you relate to the dichotomy of the battle within? I sure can. As Paul describes, there are times when our internal battle inside feels like we are losing our minds: off emotional, mental and spiritual balance. Now, add adversity to the mix, and we definitely need coping skills. The scripture below sounds like someone who is unbalanced and in need of counseling, prayer, and more counseling.

For the good that I would I do not: but the evil which I would not, that I do.

Now if I do that I would not, it is no more I that do it, but sin that dwelleth in me.

I find then a law, that, when I would do good, evil is present with me.

—Romans 7:19-21

It is an innate proclivity to fight figuratively or literally when we perceive danger because we have a built-in survival source that God gave to everything He created: the dog bites, the cat scratches, the skunk sprays, and so on. These responses to perceived danger are instinctive. To suggest that we drop our fists and raise our hands is not a posture of retreat in the context of this book. The principle encourages us to change our perceptions in order to humble ourselves, pray, and actually *allow* God to be an ever present help in our time of trouble like He promised to be. Dropping our fists and raising our hands reminds us that not every season of battle, frustration, disappointment or even righteous indignation qualifies as a reason to raise your fists.

There are times, seasons perhaps, and a myriad of circumstances, where a clenched fist, literally or metaphorically is warranted. The challenge here is knowing when to drop our fists, raise our hands to God and trust Him. Trust Him to protect us. Trust Him to give us grace. And, trust Him to move divinely in our situations.

Some people have developed an impetuous reaction to clench their emotional fists and perhaps raise their fists in response to almost every issue, concern, set back, or challenge. Every conversation becomes a debate, every correction is perceived as condemnation, and even non-threatening gestures are perceived as an attack. This behavior is not just exhibited by untrained and untamed officers killing before thinking, disgruntle terminated employees returning to their place of employment to go postal, or ignorant people exercising their right to bear arms. Some people exhibiting this behavior operate in a position that we expect and hope will provide "peace": the pastor, the teacher, the doctor, the officer, the parent, the child, the spouse, or the friend.

We are learning more everyday by the horrific tragedies we witness that people are hurting, broken, and lacking coping skills. This reality is alarming because the actions of volatile people are becoming increasingly violent. Co-workers with good tenure, students with above average grades, visitors to Bible studies, military personnel with impeccable records, famous icons of theatre, national spiritual figures, the list goes on. People, who, without provocation, just snapped.

Dropping our fists and raising our hands is a spiritual concept that can become an adopted principle to help us foster perhaps, a new response to the true battle and the one true enemy. The practice of the principle should then become our instinct and develop into our automatic response. This happens when we change our mindset. Scripture explains that behavior begins in the mind.

"Let this mind be in you, which was also in Christ Jesus."

—Philippians 2:5.

We wear gear that displays, "WWJD"—"What would Jesus do?" or preach cliché sermons about the mind and behaviors, but in order to understand the intended meaning of this one verse, we should read the whole passage of scripture to grasp the context.

Let this mind be in you, which was also in Christ Jesus:

Who, being in the form of God, thought is not robbery to be equal with God:

But made himself of no reputation, and took upon Him the form of a servant, and was made in the likeliness of men: Being found in fashion as man, He humbles Himself, and became obedient unto death, even the death of the cross.

—Philippians 2:5-8

Jesus is the model of what this concept encourages us to do. He is the embodiment of *"drop your fists and raise your hands."* His peaceable behavior was predictable but often misunderstood, and certainly underestimated. Dropping our fists and raising our hands is to respond like Jesus. He understood who He was and the power He possessed, but He humbled Himself. Do we really know who we are? Do we understand the power that we possess? When we respond to unraveling situations like Jesus did, we too will be misunderstood and underestimated. What is the misunderstanding? People often misunderstand our silence for agreement, our self-control for fear, or our meekness for weakness. What is not understood? People will often misjudge our level of empowerment. Just as the people did in Jesus' day, people will underestimate the breadth of our influence and the weight of our opinion. We are empowered. We matter. We are change-agents.

Do we realize the implications of being empowered? Those who have power, even if they have not realized it or recognized it, are often attacked. In the Bible, Adam and Eve had power and dominion over the inhabitants of the earth. We learn from their example, that, when left to our own devices, we can forfeit our divine empowerment if we habitually lose internal battles. Our internal battles are reflected in our behavior. We have been treasured with power that has a life-changing impact. Serving the Lord accentuates this power, the Spirit of the living God, given to the Believer who seeks it. The power is given to Believers for the purpose of affecting change in the world one life at a time or many at once. God has given us the best treasure, His Love, and He trusts us with it, even in our frail, broken and prone to fail lives.

But we have this precious treasure (the good news about salvation) in (unworthy) earthen vessels (of human frailty), so that they grandeur and surpassing greatness of the power will be (shown to be) from God (His sufficiency) and not from ourselves.

—2 Corinthians 4:7 (AMP)

The Battle Continues...

Temporarily broken, or all put together for a season, God empowers us to impact this world with His love, His power, His forgiveness, His grace, His mercy, and His purpose. We just need to understand that we have this power. Later in the book, we will discuss Responsible Empowerment.

The greater your sphere of influence, the greater will be your sphere of opposition. King David understood it when he explained this in Psalm 23. He wrote,

"When my enemies, even my foes rose up against me to eat up my flesh, they stumbled and fell. When war should rise against me, in this will I be confident."

The greater impact you have to change a life, the greater the persecution, the challenges, the potential for heartache, the potential for hurt, the likelihood of being falsely accused, mistaken, and the greater possibility of becoming an outcast. The Battle continues...

REFLECTIONS

Have you ever battled between your calling and your connections as a result of the call?

I have often been pulled out of situations or away from people soon after I spent time serving them in the capacity of ministry, coaching, counseling, or otherwise influencing. Sometimes, I was pulled out immediately after God added measurable value to the situation. There was no falling out or disagreement, we still maintain a loving relationship and divine connection, but I just no longer *fit in* because I am no longer *needed*. This happened so frequently that people often misunderstood the transition and felt abandoned, deserted or rejected by me, so I asked God about it. God spoke to me and simply said, "You are not meant to stay." God is so clear sometimes that we are sometimes left looking at Him like, "Soooooo, I need to leave now?" Sometimes, God is so direct, He leaves us bewildered.

There are some situations, circumstances, or people that we are called to influence but not stay connected to.

This dichotomy can be frustrating because it can mirror rejection if we are still learning how to balance our connections or if we have yet to discover our purpose in a situation. This separation is often experienced by leaders. It is probably the most challenging situation because it is perceived as rejection and does not feel good, even if there is no ill will intended. This specifically becomes awkward if *we* are the ones initiating the separation. It is important to understand the difference, however, between separation and severing. Separating is intended for a season to regroup with the ability to reengage at some point. Severing is intended to eliminate the possibility of return. In servitude, there are times when the work is complete, and there is no need to return.

Over the past three decades, I have been placed into several interesting circumstances and then seemingly snatched out of them; physically and often times emotionally. I have been taught to refer to these experiences as *divine assignments*. This is a term that is becoming widely used to explain how God uses people to add value in a particular situation that they are not necessarily meant to stay in long-term. In my endeavor to understand this concept, I believe God allowed certain situations to happen in my life to help me understand divine assignments. I have been placed into several situations that go against a culture or a "system." The *system* refers to any sense of human normalcy, formal or informal, that governs order or establishes a standard. I have lead ministries and provided oversight for churches in *systems* that do not allow women to operate in such roles. For instance, I was once asked to take on a leadership role in a church whose position was "no women pastors allowed." Well, imagine the surprise of the *naysayers* when I showed up in that role, robed up and in the pulpit, running the operations and the ministry. Many were visibly distressed and had their faces jacked up like they had just swallowed a gallon of hater aid full of sour lemons. Oh yes, they smiled in my face, but Lord did they ever gossip about me and even spread nonsensical rumors to anyone who would listen. After several tumultuous encounters, however, something broke. Till this day I am not quite sure what it was, but finally, people began to embrace me and warm up to the idea that I was the leader and not a threat to their ideologies. And right at the moment when we were *finally* in a happy place, God took me out of that situation. The Lord added value to the situation during my *assignment* and then pulled me out and placed me into the next situation.

There were times when I am sure people resented me and sometimes I was openly ridiculed in and out of these assignments. I was often invited to dinner by people just so that they could try to find out what was going on behind the scenes in my variable assignments. Once they had me among a group of people, they would begin arguing among themselves about me in my presence. One would declare that I would never serve in the capacity of pastor (while I was yet in the position) and another would retort, "Well, you see she is doing it, right?" Wow! No one asked me how I felt, what my challenges were or if they could help. We even had people show up on Sunday mornings just to watch the dynamics of the worship service. Thank God that He covered me and kept me moving so that I did not have time to focus on the haters and naysayers. Narrow-minded people were always in my rear-view mirror becoming smaller and smaller while my next venture was big, broad, and open.

I learned to ask God for His purpose as He orchestrated situations in my life and He was always faithful to show me. At some point, my prayer graduated to, "What's next Lord?" And when He led me to the next place, I would revert to, "You cannot be serious, God." Most assignments were controversial, out of human *order*, uncomfortable, out of my control and certainly not something I would choose for *myself*. I was loved and hated by the same people, and I felt as though I was in a fishbowl for all to see.

Drop your fists and raise your hands became a silent mantra for me as my personal experiences seemed to become a broadcast. On top of the inner turmoil I felt over my assignments, I was also experiencing relationship failure. Yes, right on Front Street.

I felt my life unraveling one thread at a time, and just when I thought things couldn't possibly get any worse, my father rejected me. My abusive ex would openly embarrass me in supermarkets, in front of his family, and among our acquaintances by being disrespectful, telling me that if I didn't like his abuse I could, "Get out!" The church would tabloid my life-crushing events while praying with me at the altar as I cried in anguish. I was fighting against emotional drought, mental exhaustion, and heartache. I fought against becoming depressed, dismantled, and disconnected. I would do whatever I could to prevent my daughters from reliving any of the turmoil I survived. It is impossible for our children and those closest to us to not be significantly affected by our lives, and the converse is also true; we are a part of each other, challenges, triumphs, and all.

It is also apparent that conflict and opposition seem to prey on those who are insecure and vulnerable. People with insecurities are often harboring pain by deep wounds from rejection, abuse, neglect or the perception of not being loved. Sometimes these feelings of insecurity are related to fear, guilt, shame, or the perception of personal failures. Feelings of uncertainty can also be caused by circumstances one did not choose for themselves, like being raised in an environment where there was rage, addiction, sexual assault, and other issues that people sometimes survive but never truly heal from.

Adults sometimes put children at risk for living a life with raised fists because of anxiety based upon choices and decisions they make for a myriad of reasons, such as staying in a physically abusive marriage for stability, using illicit drugs because of addiction, or engaging in illegal activities to pay for living expenses. The transference of an adult decision upon a child has generational consequences; it is not necessarily a "curse" as some would label it, but rather, a continuum of an unresolved, unhealed, or otherwise unmanaged issue.

There is a strategy often used in corporate meetings called *the parking lot method*. This approach identifies crucial issues that surface during meetings but will be addressed at a later time so that the *current* agenda can continue. Unfortunately, this strategy does not work with real life issues. There are many challenges that we would rather put into the *parking lot* category indefinitely, but that will not address or resolve anything. The longer we let our unresolved issues sit in a *parking lot*, the more they will eventually eat us alive.

It is sometimes uncomfortable to deal with the more sensitive issues that brought pain to our lives and most certainly difficult to face painful truths, like molestation, domestic violence, or public failures. I have come to realize that the freedom gained by *addressing* these issues far outweighs the heaviness of carrying the burden. The *crossroads in battle*.

Crossroads

Do you know of someone who was on their way to recovery (from a deep hurt, addiction or a behavioral pattern) but then became worse or more inflicted before they could experience deliverance and healing? This is the *crossroads in battle*.

When we are experiencing the *crossroads in battle,* opposition will attempt to take advantage of our vulnerability. The enemy uses this sensitive window of time to shatter any array of hope while someone is on their way to restoration. The enemy will target the seed of God's Word in a person's heart before it can take root. During the crossroads in battle, people tend to regurgitate the positive seeds deposited in their life. I am sure that we all know someone who has suffered in one capacity or another with repetitive cycles of failure.

This book intends to serve as a bridge between the hurt places and the other side of the hurt by helping people discover a strategy for victory. Raised fists can be literal, a propensity for physical altercation, or metaphoric: a built up mental wall, unhealthy isolation, unhealthy fear, anger, bitterness, hatred, pain, unrest, torment, anxiety, etc. The principle of dropping our fists is not meant to indicate a retreat from battle. Instead, it requires that we fight back *spiritually*, and we do this by turning to God. If we choose to trust God, we allow Him to take over the fight. As God takes the reins of our lives, we can reposition ourselves to a level of emotional strength that empowers us to overcome past hurts, forgive offenses and to move past things that made us stagnant.

Threat or Easy Prey?

Let us talk a little more about the battlefield. There are two distinct positions in battle: *threat or easy prey*. A threat is someone that is likely to cause damage or danger. Easy prey is a victim of attack who is wide open to be stolen from or destroyed. One has positioned themselves to either be a *threat* to the enemy, or his *easy prey*. Let us stop right here and understand that we are *born* as a threat to the enemy. Without going too deep into this fact, let us revisit a conversation that God had with Prophet Jeremiah.

"Before I formed thee in the belly I knew thee; and before thou camest forth out of the womb I sanctified thee; and I ordained thee a prophet unto the nations."

—Jeremiah 1:5 (KJV)

The fact that we were predestined with divine purpose is a threat to the enemy. Once we are firm in understanding that God has much more for us beyond our current situation, whether we perceive it as good or bad, we become a surmounting threat to the enemy. If we develop our relationship with Jesus Christ and begin discovering our divine destiny, this may put us into direct combat with the enemy.

Now, let us define the "enemy." The *enemy* is the devil, the fallen angel of pride, Lucifer, the deceiver of this world, who has limited time to steal, kill and destroy lives. He is the enemy of our soul who influences whoever will allow him in order to destroy others as well as themselves. It is important to know who the *real* enemy is and where the *real* battle is. It is also important to understand *what* the battle is. The battle is spiritual and happens predominately in our minds. Once we begin to understand these facts, we can change our position in the battle. Also, once we begin to change our position, we become more of a threat than easy prey to the devices of the enemy.

If we have positioned ourselves as a threat to the enemy, are we exempt from battle, from struggle, from challenges, or from heartache? Absolutely not. As we begin to recognize and depend upon the sufficiency of God, we become more susceptible to many types of opposition; however, gossip, negative opinions, ridicule and defamation of our character is less likely—because of our trust in God—to keep us bound and shackled.

People often believe that their mess-ups, struggles, and tireless efforts to live right make them easy prey to the wiles of the enemy. Did I mention that the enemy is a liar? This is a great place to discuss his traits. Lying is the enemy's primary weapon of choice. The enemy lies, and he is good at it. The *only* thing that defeats the enemy is *truth*. Because he cannot stand against truth. He will attempt to argue against it, but he has to lie to do it. He will attempt to cause us to be double-minded and confused, but he has to lie to do it. The enemy will attempt to convince us that we can never recover from a broken marriage, loss of a job, being evicted out of our home, or being kicked out of school. He may attempt to take our peace, steal our joy, and sew discord into our lives, but again, he has to *lie* to do it.

We are always a target of the enemy, and during our moments of weakness and vulnerability, God will become our strong tower and establish a strength in us to stand. This is why understanding *how* to apply the principle of *drop your fists and raise your hands* is so crucial. When we drop our fists, it is emphatically putting us into a position of empowerment—threat. To miss an opportunity to exercise our empowerment and attempt to fight back as one beating the air is tiring. It is also a waste of time. Stopping to drop our fists and raise our hands to God is powerful. This principle is a direct hit to the enemy because we are choosing the opposite of what he tries so hard to influence us to do: give up on God, lose hope, deny our faith, or to live carelessly. We are empowered as we allow God to be the source of our strength.

As threats to the enemy, we are able to minister, to encourage, and to help those going through what we have overcome. For example, if we have overcome an area in our life that once kept us defeated, we are now a threat to the enemy in that area and we can help someone experiencing the same issue. Each time we reach out to help someone overcome, we have just defeated the enemy in our life and in the life of someone else. Threat.

On the other hand, if we have *not* positioned ourselves to overcome, but run away from God in an attempt to fix things ourselves, we become *easy prey* to the enemy's attacks.

Being *easy prey* simply means that it is easy for the enemy to trip us up with lies. This happens if we depend upon outside influences to direct us, to fulfill us, and to directly impact our decisions and our destiny. As easy prey, we can sometimes find ourselves in repeated cycles and circumstances, feeling crushed, controlled, and frustrated. We want out of these cycles but we cannot seem to find our way out.

I have experienced being both a threat and easy prey. I found myself to be a threat to the enemy in some areas of my confidence and successes; however, I was also easy prey in other areas of my life where I had not totally overcome my insecurities. I allowed the perceptions and expectations of others to influence my position. Notoriety can be deceptive if it leads you away from truth and back to the *parking lot* of unresolved issues. I allowed the temporary accolades of people to make me believe that I was a consistent threat to the enemy. Well, I was a threat to the enemy in some areas; but, in other areas, I was also his easy prey. Can we be both at the same time? Most certainly.

The Lord anointed me to be effective in ministry to help others overcome and to begin to per*fect* their purpose. God allowed me to, through prayer, bring dead situations and circumstances to life for others, but I often walked away from their victory into my own defeat. I was able to help other people reconcile their relationships, find a new way to communicate to their children, and help people find new employment opportunities. At the same time, my marriage was failing, I needed to let go of ministry events to spend more time helping my kids in school, and I was hiding at work to avoid uncomfortable conversations at home. This cycle of continuing battle is what fostered this book. As I cried out to God during a season of extreme anguish in life, He softly said to me, *"Drop your fists and raise your hands."* He saw me struggling. He saw my hurt and He cared about my pain. God assured me that the battle was not mine to fight, but for Him to show Himself strong on my behalf if I would let Him. I began to journal my process and to write this book. I hope that this book will also enable you to *re-define* your position.

MEANINGFUL MOMENTS

Insecurity and deep-seeded issues of abandonment settled within me during my adolescence and early adult years. My insecurities and abandonment issues stemmed from being adopted, and after witnessing my mother's abuse at the hands of my father, they only got worse. My parents had one natural son with complications and adopted me five years later when I was two months old. I remember the disclosing conversation vividly. I was five, and busy role-playing with my Barbie dolls, when my parents sat in the high back chairs of our living room. My parents were older, in fact, old enough to be my grandparents; they were well into their careers and well established. At that time, my father was a retired Sergeant from the United States Army, the Supply Clerk for the army base, and he owned a barber shop across town. My mother was a specialized Critical Care Registered Nurse in the Intensive Care Unit at the army hospital. Both of my parents were raised in poor environments and amid racism. My parents were practical, discrete, rather formal, and spoke to my brother and I very direct, never using "baby-talk" or nick-names. Even though I was very young, I sensed that something was different in their tone. I put my favorite doll down and waited, sitting in front of them like a student. Each of them took turns giving me information about my adoption. They spoke to me as if I was able to comprehend the information. Of course I had plenty of questions. I asked what adoption meant, why my mother did not keep me, and if that meant that I was not their baby. I was a rather precocious child, so, the first day back to school after this conversation, I shared my new *stuff* during "Show and Tell." My parents received a call from the school asking if the information I shared was true because, apparently, I recited this wonderful new story with details, probably adding some flare. Over the years, those questions did not stop but became more mature in nature. I learned that my birth mother chose to make my adoption a *"closed case."* She provided a lot of non-identifying information, like physical descriptions, ethnicity, culture, and family dynamics. I learned that my birth parents were attending the same prestigious university at the time she learned that she was pregnant with me. She said that she and my father were only children to older parents who could not take care of me. According to the information provided by her, my father was Creole, and his mother was prejudice against Blacks, overbearing and controlling. My father apparently dropped out of college and went into the military to provide for me, but died shortly after joining the military. My father's death, his mother's attitude and her desire to finish college, were the reasons my mother gave for making the adoption a "closed case."

Despite my curiosity about my birth parents, I felt loved and adored by my adoptive parents. My life was normal and happy for most of the childhood, but then, at the impressionable age of 12, my whole life changed. My father—my Hero, my Protector and my Provider, became my biggest nightmare. My loving and doting daddy became overtly abusive in our home. Our place of comfort turned into a house of terror when my father became heavily involved with drugs and alcohol. He was functional, kept up perfect professional and social appearances, but from that age until 17, I did not know how I would be awakened every morning. My father's vehement railings, cursings, door-slamming, and sometimes, physical assaults, became my alarm clock. We lived with a terrorist for several years.

To the public, we were progressive; the only Blacks in an all-White neighborhood, middle-class, living within walking distance of the best schools, but behind that wonderful front was a house of horrors. My father still provided and never allowed his proclivities to interfere with the management of the household from my vantage point. My brother and I began using marijuana and alcohol when I was only 12 and he was 17. I believe that beyond experimenting and recreation, we were also masking the fear we lived with at home. My mom picked up two jobs on the side just to stay out of dodge.

In the midst of this dynamic, my brother and I were accomplished students and athletes. Outside of the home, we were cheerful, fun, loving, and full of life. Our family and close friends had no idea my father was abusive; however, they knew he was strict and at times, would embarrass us in front of company. Dad was more verbally abusive to my brother than he was physically because my brother was at his eye level and had already grabbed the belt when he was 12 years old. My discipline seemed reasonable until my father lost his rationality. One night, he came home from the club and let out what seemed to be all of his frustrations and anger from childhood onto my body with his leather belt. When my mother came home from work after midnight, she could hear me in my room still crying and wrestling in my covers trying to get comfortable from all of the whelps and bruises on my legs and back. When she saw my body, she covered her mouth in terror, took me downstairs, lifted up my pajamas, and showed my father what he did to my body. She told him that would be the last time he would put his hands on me in anger. I did not dress out for physical education that entire week to avoid questions, or worse, a home visit from Child Protective Services.

I became a born again Christian at 15, serving in the church heavily, but my brother continued to binge on drugs and alcohol.

As I grew into a young adult, I became involved in abusive relationships. Because of my father, I had always been a defender of my friends against bullies. Although protecting my friends gave me a sense of justice, not being able to protect my mother in the same way weighed heavily on me; especially, as I watched my father's emotional mutilation of her morph into disfiguring, physical abuse.

I left home at 17. Not because I wanted to, but because I was forced to. One day after church, I sensed my father working himself into one of his rages. I started whistling some Gospel music so that he wouldn't realize I was discreetly trying to leave the house. My plan, however, did not work. The moment I neared the door, there he was, spewing his venom. Being the good Christian girl I was at the time I decided to help him. I told him how much psychological and spiritual help he needed and even attempted to openly rebuke Satan from his mind. My father did not appreciate my "advice," and illustrated this fact by knocking me out cold. When I came to, I was face down on the floor. Unfortunately, we had out of town company visiting during this event. My maternal grandmother just prayed and watched silently in tears. My cousin picked me up off of the floor. My eye was slightly bruised. After I stood up, I let my father know that I was leaving. He snatched my car keys out of my hand and said that I could not drive the car because he bought it. I responded that he obviously felt that he could take my life too since he bought it as well, then I walked out. I walked to the nearest payphone and called my mother at work. She left work and took me to the Police Station while my face was bruised. I asked the police officer to have a discussion with my father, but not to take him into custody because it would make my mother's life miserable at home. The officer indicated that the police department does not provide that type of intervention and that if he went to the house, he would take him into custody for battery. Scared for my mother's safety, especially with me leaving home, I elected not to pursue this end. I went home and packed some clothes. When we arrived at the house, my father had his drug friends there, smoking and drinking. He began railing and spitting out nasty remarks. As we were leaving, my father pushed my mother and she almost fell. I told him that I loved him but that he needed to get some professional help. He told me that he loved me too.

I left home that day and did not return until I came back to announce that I was getting married to a local juvenile delinquent who, at that time, was also a best friend. He was the only one who knew of the horrible dreams that awakened me every night. In these recurring nightmares, I was always fighting my father (to keep him away from my mother), and right before he killed me or I killed him, I would wake up. These dreams lasted over a decade.

During this time, I was attending a local community college, working and applying for universities to transfer into. I was accepted to several universities further from home, but I chose one closer just in case I needed to rush home to protect mom.

The day after I turned 20, still playing with Barbie dolls, still a virgin, and on my way to college, I married the delinquent. My best friend —My Escape. I only wanted us to be roommates; however, his father was a Pastor and convinced my mother marriage was best to avoid inappropriate perceptions and unwanted pregnancies out of wedlock. We were dating, but we were not physically intimate. Nevertheless, we married. Bad mistake for so many obvious reasons, but I needed to *escape* home and I was afraid to be alone with the nightmares. So, I escaped those nightmares to create new ones of my own. Mr. Escape matriculated from a juvenile delinquent into an adult delinquent and quickly became an abusive spouse.

It is amazing how people stay in abusive situations because they refuse to let go of a dream. They hope that it will get better somehow if they just hold on.

People who abuse others do not love themselves, and for this cause, the situation may never get better. When people endure abuse over a length of time, they may begin not to love themselves. Perhaps I did not love myself enough to get out of my abusive marriage.

Thinking back, Mom probably became numb and stopped focusing on herself, much less consider loving herself. She was raised in a poor environment and worked hard to obtain an education and to reach her family and career goals. During her formative years, mom cleaned houses and served the United States Army to pay for nursing school and to send money back home to her younger siblings. Her dream was to have the "white picket fence" lifestyle; a home, a husband, two kids, a dog, and financial stability. She achieved her dreams, but at a horrific expense from my vantage point. She had the material aspects of her dream, but she forfeited a merry heart. My mother stayed in a volatile marriage and I am not sure that she actually knew the impact it would have on me as I watched in terror and sometimes horrific fear. Like my mother, I found out that forfeiting a merry heart was the recipe for becoming easy prey to the enemy. The consequences of being easy prey had dire consequences for me: I lived a life of raised fists, was always threatened by loud noises (thinking they were an indication of progressing rage), and felt constantly compelled to look over my shoulder to block blows that sometimes never came.

Yes, I asked God where He was in all of this. I even cursed at Him when I was going through it. Free will and free choice is a double-edged sword. God let me know that I was in a real family, with real issues, but that He was a real God and I could trust Him.

Thank God this was not the end of my story. God truly is an ever present help in our time of trouble. Even in troubled times, we are the enemy's worse nightmare because God's strength is made perfect in our weakness.

If we are living to obey God, we are a definite threat to the enemy, *even* with raised fists. We may conquer some battles and may win some wars, but to become a consistent victor, we must learn how to draw our unwavering weapon against the enemy: the ability to "*drop our fists and to raise our hands.*" Right in the midst of a trial, before you enter conflict, as you are faced with a decision, as you go through your storms, when you are hurt, frustrated, confused, in crisis, and you are right on the verge of a major breakthrough; this is when you draw the weapon of this principle.

I know it sounds suicidal and dangerous. The idea of dropping any weapon in the midst of battle sounds ludicrous to the natural ear, but God has another weapon within us, and when the heat of battle is at its peak, we drop our natural weapons and everything that goes against the norm and begin to Worship. This is the essence of the principle. It means to rely and totally depend on

God to defy the natural you and allow Jesus to work through you supernaturally. This is accomplished through worshipping God. It is not a normal position in the height of battle, so it requires humility, submission, focus, and surrender to God's power and ever presence.

We sing songs about God's ever-present power and His omniscience and omnipotence. We believe that God is Jehovah Jireh (The Lord is my Provider), Jehovah Nissi (The Lord is my Banner) and Jehovah Shalom (The Lord is my Peace), El Shaddai (All sufficient), and El Elyon (God Most High). However, when it rains adversity in our lives, we hide behind our fists.

Prophet Isaiah said that when the enemy comes in like a flood, the Spirit of God promises to raise a standard against him. A flood, like a tormenting rain, is intended to destroy. A *flood* is an outpouring of a relentless tidal wave of water, coming from all directions, with the ability to take everything out in its path. But God declared that a standard will be lifted that would set up a spiritual damn against the flood. The standard He raises is IN us. Our supernatural overtakes our natural, and we operate in a sense of peace that surpasses onlookers' understanding and even our own understanding at times.

If you are a Worshiper, you are a threat to the kingdom of darkness. Now is the perfect time to experience this level of worship. Get to a quiet place where you are alone with God. Lift your heart to Him and say from within,

"God, I surrender myself to you; my mind, my heart and all that is within me that has the proclivity to fight you, intentionally and perhaps without intent. God I recognize that you love me in spite of what I have done or who I have become, and I need you to raise Your standard in my life. I need you to do in and for me what I cannot do for myself. I choose to trust You, to believe You and to be still. I am dropping my fists, and I raise my heart, my hands and my being to you; now, in the name of Jesus."

Armor On

Put on all of God's armor so that you will be able to stand firm against all strategies of the devil.

—Ephesians 6:11

Within the arsenal described in Ephesians, I felt like I most needed the helmet of salvation, although all components are essential. I needed protection for my mind.

It is important for people to know that they have a right to be safe. It is difficult to convince a victim of abuse that we do not have to live in fear, anger, or in torment. It is challenging to convince a victim of abuse that we can fight back with proper tools and resources. It is even harder to get a victim out of an abusive environment where we may feel trapped. If we conquer that battle in our lives, we can help put on an amour that will defeat the lies of the enemy.

It is important to put on God's armor and not raise our *own* fists because His armor is governed by Him and can without a doubt, defeat the enemy. We are not told to take off our earrings, put on brass knuckles, or grease our faces. We are told to put truth on like a belt, righteous thinking, and right living as a breastplate, covering our heart. We are also told to put peace and readiness to share God's love on like shoes. After these things, we are told to armor ourselves with faith like a shield, instead of fists, and to wear God's perspective on our head like a helmet. Finally, we are told to carry a weapon, a sword, the Bible. This is the amour we should wear in the battle we fight.

The battle continues, but the way we fight it will *not* if we apply the principles and trust God for the outcome.

CHAPTER BREAK

CHAPTER 2
THE HIT LIST

It is important that we know our life is safe with God. It is important to understand that the enemy desires to sift us as wheat and to ultimately destroy our relationship with God and with others. It is important to understand and to know these facts so that we will not drown under the manifold hits the enemy will attempt upon our lives.

Jesus warned his disciples of the Hit List, and He is yet warning us today.

"Simon, Simon, Satan has asked to sift you all of you as wheat. But I have prayed for you, Simon, that your faith may not fail."

—Luke 22:31 (NIV)

We have heard the term "Hit List" in gangster movies and TV shows such as *The God Father*, *The Sopranos*, *American Gangster*, and *Training Day* to name a few. What is a Hit List? It is an identified list of people or things selected as the object of a certain treatment or course of action. The Online Slang Dictionary defines the Hit List as simply *a list of people to murder*. The cause of such action can be for a myriad of reasons but is mostly political. The film industry depicts the conspiracy and drama involved in carrying out a "hit" on a particular person or persons of interest. The enemy of our souls does the same thing. He enlists people to work with him, even though they may not realize it, to take people of interest out of the way.

Who are the people he targets? He targets the people that he perceives to be a threat to his agenda. He targets the people that have the potential and the capacity to derail him and to defeat him by exposure. When we identify his lies and help others to dismantle his lies upon their life, we are in his way. If you are a catalyst for change, you become a target of the enemy because you are empowered to shift situations.

A *catalyst for change* is an influential person who can cause permanent change, either in someone's life or a particular situation, with unusual speed. This means that when you step into someone's life or enter a circumstance that is in turmoil, your presence changes the atmosphere *quickly* and *permanently*. You may say something that changes a mindset, a perception, policy, or an established system. You may not have to say anything at all because by definition, *you* are the change agent.

You may not have a special title or position of authority. Influence is not predicated upon what you are, but your influence is based on *who* you are. People are tolerated and sometimes heard based upon *what* they are, meaning, what position or title they have. But people trust, embrace, appreciate and follow someone because of *who* they are. Being a *catalyst for change* implies that God has divinely anointed you with empowerment. Everybody with power is not responsible. Being a divine catalyst for change may be a lot to take in because it requires something of you. It requires you to respond. The notion that we can actually cause capitol change is loaded with responsibility. To whom much is given, much is required.

There is a demonic Hit List for those with empowerment, whether they have fully recognized or actualized their empowerment or not. But just because the weapon forms, does not mean that it shall prosper.

"No weapon that is formed against you will succeed; And every tongue that rises against you in judgment you will condemn. This is the heritage of the servants of the Lord. And this is their vindication from Me," says the Lord.

—*Isaiah 54:17 (AMP)*

We essentially have one enemy; however, he will manifest in many ways: through people, within circumstances, and within systems.

He is the same enemy that opposed God and the people of God from the beginning. Jesus referred to him as Satan, the prince of the air and an angel of light coming to deceive the hearts of man. According to scripture, he was Lucifer, the preferred beautiful angel of praise and worship in Heaven. He was even over the choir. Mercy! But because of his wickedness and pride, he and the host of imps that followed him were kicked out of Heaven.

Just as he opposes God, he opposes all those whom God creates, and specifically those who have responded to God's divine call for His will and purpose. The enemy hates God's people and will stop at nothing to destroy them, but he has limitations: permission, resources and time. The enemy is subject to God, cannot move in spite of God, and is controlled by God.

Once we truly understand this, we have leverage to defeat the enemy from having a foothold in our lives or the lives of those we touch. The principle of *drop your fists and raise your hands* is one that will teach us how to conquer the enemy that is busy trying to put us in entanglements that distract and disconnect us from God, people, and positive choices.

We will learn how to stop allowing our emotions to rise to every occasion. We will understand how to surrender to Jesus Christ before battles, in the midst of battles, and once the battles are conquered. Why the battle? Why the fight? Why the hurt? Why the fiery darts of the enemy?

The genuine condition of something or someone is exposed when it is put under pressure, under fire, or under siege. In some cases, you can see right through an object by subjecting it to fire. God allows conflict in our lives for purification, penetration, preparation, and for a purpose. It is in the process of our hearts being *tried* that we can apply *Drop Your Fists and Raise Your Hands*. A heart or mind is *tried* when it is challenged by adversity, pain and the temptation to give up, but continues to overcome and rise above obstacles. A tried heart and mind is one that should be able to be trusted.

David often invited God to *try* his heart again and again and then search his heart yet *again*. David was inviting God to see if he could handle challenges that threatened his faith and his integrity. In some cases, David failed, and he would then ask God to give him a clean heart. This is the process of purification: inviting God to make sure we are in alignment with His will and with our purpose.

Going through a humiliating situation opens our heart to be penetrated by the truth. Some people will never overcome foolish pride until they face a crisis that forces them to drop their fists or even get on their knees. This is the process of *truth penetration.* The truth is more readily received when it is the *only* alternative. Sometimes God allows the situations in our life to bring us low, break us down and bruise us deep so that we will reach out to Him for the truth He has been trying to get us to see.

God will also prepare us for His provision. If the provision is already established, why do we need to be prepared for it? I am learning that God's provision is not dependent upon us, but can be delayed by our foolishness. God prepares our hearts to prevent foolish pride, arrogance, waste and perversion. Remember, blessings in the heart of a fool can be dangerous. God will sometimes allow the billows of life to prepare our hearts to remain humble right before He gets ready to overtake us with His best.

Our purpose is often the diamond in the rough from our tough experiences. David expressed this well when he concluded that it was good for him to be afflicted so that he could pay attention to God's truths. If we never go through setbacks, we will not experience overcoming. If we are never sick, we will not experience healing. If we never get caught up in entanglements or trapped in the bondage of our failure, we may never experience deliverance.

But He said unto me, "My grace is sufficient for you, for my power is made perfect in weakness."

—2 Corinthians 12:9

Paul endured an issue that the Bible never reveals. The Bible only records that Paul asked God to remove the "thorn in his flesh" several times before God answered him. Independent, wealthy, educated, and influential, Paul would have to depend upon God's grace in his time of weakness. God will challenge our faith, ground our faith, and cause us to put our faith into action by the use of a thorn. I don't have to ask if you have identified your thorn because I have no doubt you have been trying to remove it for quite some time now. God will also allow us to reject seeds of His Word until we become famished and dehydrated enough that we allow divine seeds to take root, germinate, and become permanent attributes in our lives. God's grace is truly sufficient for the conflicts in our life.

The threats and actual grazes we experience from being on the Hit List teach us valuable life lessons and helps to prevent catastrophic consequences. Sometimes we struggle with a physical ailment, chronic aches and pains, or other debilitating issues. We may pray and ask God to take it away, but He may respond by only lessening the pain without removing the "thorn." Some may experience the loss of a loved one: a child, a spouse, a parent, or a best friend. These are emotional thorns, and it may take some time to recover from the sting of the pain, but God promises that His grace will be enough to cover the hurt and to repair the broken place.

Christians are obviously not the only target for the enemy's Hit List because we are not the only population who are catalysts for change or in positions of authority. The enemy is seeking to destroy anyone or any movement that will impact or influence people or policies in a positive or progressive direction, especially when these movements are motivated by love. Works motivated by love will ignite the adversary to go to great lengths to derail and destroy.

What do the weapons on the Hit List look like? There are multiple and sometimes multi-layered trials we face: disappointments, broken promises, shattered dreams, painful memories, financial struggles, marital problems, false friends, abusive parents, abusive spouses, abusive children, loneliness, addiction, bad habits and, of course, the many lies the enemy tells us. These are the weapons the enemy uses to barricade us from peace, joy, deliverance and healing.

We are pressured in every way (hedged in), but not crushed; perplexed (unsure of finding a way out), but not driven to despair; hunted down and persecuted, but not deserted (to stand alone); struck down, but never destroyed.

—2 Corinthians 4:8-9

These are the weapons that keep our fists raised and keep us in fear of dropping them to raise our hands to God.

These are the weapons of mass destruction that sometimes bring years of torment. These are the weapons that cause depression, anxiety, stress, ulcers, disorders, disease, and even suicide.

These are the weapons that we shall defeat as we drop our fists and raise our hands.

Let's review an example of a Monarch of Faith that people often refer to and relate to when they are experiencing a heavy burden; Job, one of the heroes described in the Bible.

God gave Satan authority to attempt to corrupt Job. We know the story of how God had a conversation with Satan and asked him what he was up to. Satan must give an account to God because he is totally and entirely subject to and controlled by God. Of course, Satan responded that he had been going up and down earth seeking whom he could devour. God asked him if he had considered His Servant Job. Satan had been watching Job but when he saw God's hedge of protection around him, he left Job alone. Have you ever felt like God unleashed the enemy to try you to the end of yourself? I have, and guess what? I believe that once we come to the end of "us," we will totally embrace Him. As soon as God gave the enemy permission to attack Job within parameters, the enemy put Job on his Hit List, trying to cause him to denounce his faith in God and to lose his right mind and curse God to his face. The enemy used Job's closest friends, his wife, the death of his children, and the destruction of his financial stability to put a "hit" on his life.

What has the enemy used to threaten your faith? Close friends? A significant other? The death of someone close? Stability? Or more importantly, what will God use to allow the enemy to threaten, take away or destroy to get your attention? Sorry, I just had to go there.

I can relate to how Job may have felt, but I have not always been as successful in my responses. Because of this, God allowed many attention-getting hits to threaten my life. Through this, I embraced the principle to drop my fists and raise my hands.

MEANINGFUL MOMENTS

Have you ever felt that when God kicked the enemy and his imps out of Heaven, they landed right on top of you? Yeah, me too.

My Escape developed into an adult delinquent, a wannabe gangster, and an abuser. He began using drugs, harboring drug paraphernalia and loaded weapons and would parade stray women in and out of our home. If I challenged him, he would tell me to "Get out" right in front of whoever was present. That became his mantra to me for several years.

After I had finished my undergraduate program, I was ready to have a child, but in this chaos? I did not believe in divorce and figured I was stuck, so I was initially determined to just make the best of it. Realizing that I would be repeating a dangerous cycle if I brought a child into a volatile marriage, I went to the doctor seeking birth control only to find out that we were expecting. I was overjoyed with excitement yet scared. I poured my focus on the blessing to come while his behavior became relentless with abuse, deception and adultery.

I did not like guns, especially loaded guns in the house, so when he caught me trying to unload one of his guns in the baby's nursery, he proceeded to fight me while I was eight months pregnant. When he tackled me to the floor, I felt the gun barrel on my belly, so I let go. He left our house and went to his girlfriend's (he lived there while I was pregnant). He would only come home to change clothes every morning before work. The Hit List!

I was able to keep this living condition I found myself in away from my parents for quite some time because we lived 65 miles away. By my third trimester, I developed life-threatening preeclampsia and gestational diabetes which brought my mother to town for frequent visits. During one of my doctor appointments, while mom was visiting, the doctor confronted me about my worsening condition because she could see that it was exacerbated by something I refused to share. I confessed the abuse while my mother listened with tears streaming down her face. The doctor told my mom that my living conditions were threatening me and the baby's life. Mom became fully aware of the flagrant affair, neglect, and attempts at physical abuse. Notice I said *attempts* at physical abuse.

A person who survives the kind of abuse I experienced in my parent's home is not a good match for an abusive mate. People who are under constant threat live with raised fists and, over time, we build up emotional strength and courage and eventually, we fight back. Therefore, physical abuse was attempted but quickly depleted from his arsenal. Hubby dearest quickly learned not to go there with me because I let him know and provided evidence that I would survive by *any* means necessary. Over time I lost who I was and became who I had to be in order to survive.

When the threat on me and my baby's life began to cause frequent and extensive hospital stays due to the stress of the emotional and verbal abuse, my mother attempted to plead with my husband while I was not present and asked him to lay aside whatever differences we had until we were out of harm's way. She asked him not to leave me alone at night because I could go into convulsions in my sleep and die or lose the baby. He lied to her of course and promised to be there. When she called the next night to check on me and asked to speak to him, I told her that he was at his other home with his girlfriend. My mother, well, you can imagine her heartache.

Mom took me and my baby home from the hospital because he refused to wait for us to be discharged. He was fired from his job the day our daughter was born. I became the only provider for a period and because I spent weeks in and out of the hospital prior to our daughter being born, I fell behind on bills. We received a final notice on the water bill, and since I was on bed rest, I gave My Escape the money to make the payment and prevent disconnection. Not only did he not pay the bill, he disappeared for several days. I had to bathe my newborn baby with the hot and cold water from an Alhambra water cooler until I could pay the bill. God never fails! A few months after our daughter was born, I began to find evidence that my life and her life could be in danger. I found his three pagers, drug paraphernalia, condoms, and notes with witchcraft symbols. I began to have a recurrent dream that he and a female figure were standing over me wearing black hoods. I would wake up just as they began to walk away with my baby. After these incidents, I found his loaded gun, the same one he fought me over while I was pregnant, and put it in my mattress in between me and my baby's bassinet. I realized that I was fighting the devil and whatever spirit had jumped into his mind and the mind of his girlfriend. If the dreams I had were a warning of an attempt for them to take my life to steal my baby, I would be ready. Interestingly enough, I had this gun in place for several weeks. I would see him come home and look frantically for it, but he never asked me if I had it or if I knew where it was. I would quietly watch him pace and search as I read a book, nursed the baby or watched TV. The day he found the gun under my mattress is the day he left. When I came home from work, he told me that it was time for him to leave because he no longer knew who I was or what I would do. I told him that was a good idea because I didn't know either.

Ten months after our daughter was born, while he was incarcerated, My Escape and his girlfriend had a son and he demanded that the child be named after him. He made sure to contact me from prison on a three-way call to give me the news. The Hit List!

The abuse, the betrayal and the danger were all a series of fist-raising events in my life, but God protected me and hid me. I "escaped" from him while he was incarcerated and moved on with my life as a divorced, yet free and single parent.

I fell into a deep depression, went astray for a season, and even contemplated suicide, but God's grace carried me and rescued me until I returned back to Him by attending a Holiness church. I needed an IV-drip ministry to bring me back into my right mind and to restore my relationships. I needed to be strong for my baby girl, but I was broken, vulnerable and weak. It was then that God hid me while he put the fragments of my broken life back together and strengthened me.

After what seemed like a never-ending season of my father's monster-streak and the abuse by My Escape, I was emotionally and otherwise burnt out, exhausted, and numb. After a decade had passed, my mother's health failed (she had suffered from a rare auto-immune disease over 30 years), and she became bed-ridden. While my mother was dying, my father became even more abusive towards her. During one of my visits with her, she asked me to pray that she die. She was tired, scared, and lost her desire to live. That was my cue to do something, so I took a leave of absence from work, packed up everything, including my daughter, and moved in with them to shield her. By then, my father knew not to hurt her on my watch, well not physically anyway. My mother and I became survivors, prayer partners, and confidantes for each other because we could not talk to anyone else. We were fugitives on the enemy's Hit List because together, we kept dodging bullets and other threats.

While I stayed there for a while, my father was, on some level, in-check and clearly resented my bodyguard role in his house. I watched him closely, and if my mother had a need, I would make sure to let him know, and he would curse under his breath, but he became very attentive to her needs. One day, he told me I would never marry again because no man could measure up and handle me. I think he may have meant this as a compliment, but I took it as an insult because I no longer trusted him. There was so much damage to our relationship due to his abuse. I had lost respect for him, and it was evident. He would often mention to my mother, in my earshot, that he did not appreciate the way I looked at him.

Mom's health eventually got so bad that she was hospitalized. She could not breathe on her own and was put on life support, which was not her desire. After a few days, the family was brought in to make a decision. This created division among us. My father panicked and decided that he wanted everything done to extend her life, with or without quality. My brother fought to take her off life support, knowing that she did not want to be resuscitated. When the doctor looked at me for my opinion, before I could adequately respond, my brother became belligerent and asked how could I have an opinion since I was not even her natural child. Wow! My father was in tears, the doctor, who knew my mother for over 30 years, was surprised. He said that my mother and he were very close and that she never shared that I was adopted; therefore, my opinion was taken into consideration. I expressed that my mother was a Christian and ready to die in peace; however, because my father was her husband of 37 years, I supported his decision. My brother cursed out everyone in the room, including the doctor, and stormed out. It took over 10 years for the relationship between my brother and father to heal after this incident. Mom was eventually taken off life support and succumbed to the heart and lung disease that had taken over her body.

After mom passed, I truly felt alone. I began to desire companionship, but my father's words about no man being able to measure up and handle me had really caused me to doubt myself. I gave myself one year to prove him wrong. Living with my parents before mom passed helped me to get out of debt, establish some savings, and have more free time. I had become self-sufficient and resilient.

I was on a mission to find someone easy and nice this time. I even had an inappropriate mantra for the madness: "All I need is an extra set of hands and a middle knee because I got everything else." Really? Bad! All bad! This is an example of how raised fists can cloud our perceptions and distort good judgment.

Be careful what you look for when you are in a hurry. Don't let an outside voice of perception poison muffle your inner voice. Be careful about what you seek when you are broken hearted. It is best not to make any sudden moves or life-changing decisions until you can do so with a level head.

Of course, I got just what I asked for. Within one year, I was introduced to my "Salve." It was refreshing to have a nice man in my life after all the negative male drama I had experienced. Salve was easy on the eyes and pleasant. We fell in love and within one year, we married. The following year, we had a daughter.

By definition, a salve is what we use to protect an injury, an open wound. It is a balm, used to soothe, ease the pain, and provide comfort to a wound without actually healing the wound or treating the cause of the wound.

So there I was, making a permanent plan out of a temporary pacifier. A salve is only intended to make an open wound feel better temporarily. I applied much salve because my wound was deep.

I learned quickly that temporary is just that. From my vantage point, my Salve temporarily kept a stable job, temporarily told the truth, was not good with money, had deep-seeded and unresolved issues, and temporarily needed me to survive. When he met someone that he felt was a leg up, he methodically planned an exodus and set the wheels in motion to move on. It appears that Salve could not handle the terrain of commitment because he was only the two extra hands and middle knee that I sought and caught. My salve wore off before our daughter was one, leaving an unhealed wound much bigger. Salve confessed that he had fallen into a deep depression during my third trimester of pregnancy, but he refused therapy and rejected counseling. I, again, almost lost my life and the life of our daughter due to preeclampsia exacerbated by the stress in our marriage. Our daughter was eight months old when Salve announced he was leaving. It was a Sunday morning, and the girls and I were already dressed for church. At first, I thought he meant he was going to visit his older daughter from a previous marriage, but he clarified that he was, in fact, leaving me, leaving *us*. He said that he was moving in with a woman who promised to take care of him and that he would not need to work for a while. He said that would be easier. I asked him how he could easily consider leaving his family to move in with another woman when he knew that we needed him. His mind was made up and he seemed relieved. Really??

I stayed gone long enough for him to pack up and leave. When we got home from church, I saw that he had taken some things but left a lot behind. I began to fold up the remains, pack them in boxes, and line them up. He returned three days later, attempting to conjure up a conversation to justify his actions and found all of his belongings near the door. He attempted to start an argument stating that he was leaving because it was too hard trying to keep a job, trying to take care of his family and because he believed I wanted him to choose between his older daughter and me. We had already discussed these issues before (and close friends and counselors had tried to convince him that his notions were not true). On this day; however, I did not have to say a word. I simply opened the door, and immediately, he began taking his things out. We may be on a hit list, but sometimes, we need to return fire.

I endured a lengthy court battle with torturous emotional strain, but God gave me favor with the judge and favor in the child support process! God moved by His power in the court room, specifically on the final day of court. The Judge, known for being brutal and harsh, openly spoke words of encouragement to me to the extent that even the court reporter was in tears. The Judge actually apologized for the pain that he saw I had endured. He said that I had been taken advantage of and that I would recover beyond this painful experience. He ordered Salve to pay back expenses and wished me luck for my future. God is ever present in the battle, even when we feel strengthless. After leaving the courtroom that day I drove a little past the building and had to pull over because I was crying so much I could not see.

Unfortunately, winning the court and custody battle and being compensated with child support did not lower my emotional fists because I was hurting. In the midst of this process, can you believe I never stopped teaching or preaching? The truth is, I thought I would never stop crying either.

After this ordeal, when God would remind me to drop my fists and raise my hands, I thought, "To get sucker punched—I don't think so!" I did not drop my fists at that time, nor did I raise my hands. But I kept preaching. Things that make you go *hmmm*.

Back to the story of Job...

Unlike most of us, Job did not bring his peril upon himself. Through much anguish and despair, Job's response was to drop his fists and raise his hands. When the enemy's attempt upon Job's character came back void, the enemy took a portion of job's health and strength. The only reason he could not kill Job is because God restricted his access and gave him a boundary. The conclusion of the story? Job received complete restoration and an over abundance of return *because* he dropped his fists and raised his hands.

This is a vivid example of Satan's desire against all of us. Thank God *He* restricts his access. God promises not to put more on us than we can bear, although sometimes, we may not agree with God's perspective of our bearing capacity.

All of the issues we face that threaten our peace have been the enemy's attempt to go beyond his restricted access. The enemy uses any and all avenues to destroy our faith, incriminate our reputation, and mutilate our influence. As illustrated in my Meaningful Moments, the enemy's most effective weapon to use against us is ourselves. If he can take us off our game by using our open doors, he can draw us away from our center. Open doors are the emotional pathways we leave open to our hearts and causes us to be vulnerable and an easy target for the enemy. We are told to protect our heart because it is our center, the central headquarters to who we are. It is our Command Center. If we keep the door of our heart ajar, the enemy creeps in and tries to infiltrate. Our heart is the key to our emotions, our filter (where we process incoming information), our lens (our perspective) and our outpour (what comes out of our heart through our mouth).

Above all else, guard your heart, for everything you do flows from it.

—Proverbs 4:23(NIV)

What we *feel* impacts our thought process and our inner truth (belief system). Our filters spawn from our feelings. We process incoming information through this filter. If the filter is not washed with truth from the Word of God from positive reinforcements, we begin to limit our capacity because our filters are not clear of debris like CHAFF and TARES. We will discuss those elements a little bit later in this chapter.

Our perspective either allows to see *beyond* "right now" or *limits* us to only see "today" without considering the big picture. Density of our lens will limit us to near-sightedness, keeping everything compact without room for growth. We need to be able to see the intangible, and this is accomplished by faith, in faith, and through faith. Our lens either stirs up a hunger for what is not seen or it restricts our vision to what is right in front of us.

For we live by faith, not by sight.

—2 Corinthians 5:7

If there were nothing new, seemingly unreachable, or incredibly challenging, our potential outpour would be limited. Our outpour is a direct reflection of our dreams, hunger, and expectations. God is always challenging us to enlarge, stretch, and expect beyond our reach. Our dreams are divine preambles of what could be and what shall be if we have faith and take action. Our hunger is the driving force that bridges the gap between our dreams and the manifestation of our expectations. Hunger compels and propels because if we are hungry enough for what we want, we will stop at nothing to make it happen. People become creative when they are hungry enough. The enemy wants to keep us withdrawn, not just shut-in emotionally, but without the ability to see abroad. Thinking bigger can cause an almost instinctive reaction to raise up our fists if we allow the enemy to intimidate our desire to reach. But hunger will overcome any intimidation.

Let's challenge our lens and open our outpour. The exercise below will allow us to revisit or perhaps visit for the first time, our dreams, aspirations, ideas and passions.

EXERCISE #2
PUT A DATE ON IT

This exercise is an opportunity to discover or to rediscover dreams. We will accomplish this exercise in 3 phases.

Phase I: Name three things that you want to do, wanted to do, and believe you would still do if you could focus on it, had time to pursue it or felt motivated to get started?

Example: Finish Writing a Book

Now, come up with at least one for yourself. Your list can be as complex as completing a dissertation or as simple as setting up a monthly budget.

1. _____

2. _____

Phase II: Set your date for completion

Allow a possibility to become your reality by making it a goal and objective. There are, however, rules to setting goals and objectives; they must be *measurable*, and should be achievable.

Some of our goals may stretch us to think outside the box and to reach beyond our comfort zone.

I have provided a sample goal and objective to help you with this exercise.

Example: Finish writing the book by March 2017

- Submit total manuscript to an Editor by Jan 31
- Approve Cover Design by Feb 15
- Submit for Publication by Apr 1
- Production and Marketing by Apr 15

Phase III: Deliverables

- Once you put a date on the completion, set and date the associated tasks required to reach each goal.
- This provides you with the plan to execute and also puts the work in motion.
- We can modify and push dates out if necessary, but we cannot stop moving.
- This establishes accountability.

And the Lord answered me: "Write the vision; make it plain on tablets, so they may run who reads it."

—Habakkuk 2:2

The Intent of the Hit List

The Hit List is not just about hurting our feelings, inflicting self-esteem wounds, or taking away security; it is also about limiting our expansion, diminishing our destiny, and poisoning our thought process to squelch our purpose. This is why a new strategy has to be developed within us. We cannot continue to fight the way we have in the past. We have to come to the place where we raise our hands. It is *here,* that our empowerment can take a significant turn. But we must first pass through the process of dropping our fists.

Dropping our fists may bring us to the bridge of a major thoroughfare that we all wish to avoid – public display. The enemy attempts to display our shame and embarrassment. This is what kept my fists raised even when I was weary. Everyone was looking. It took time before I thought about it and decided, "So what!" I had to realize that my inner voice should *always* be louder than the voice of the crowd. I began to help others realize what I discovered: the enemy works *for* us while working against us. The noise of the tabloids provides confirmation of how important I am. When the tabloids are silent, I have to check my pulse.

Tabloids are simple folk who love to gossip. People with tabloid tendencies are reduced to living their lives through the perceived challenges of others. They have locked themselves into keeping track of the goings-on of others, so every now and again, I pose for them from my *best* side.

"The thief cometh not, but for to steal, to kill and to destroy."

—John 10:10 (KJV)

Jesus explained the intent of the enemy. He called him a thief. But he's not just trying to ruin our financial stability, mess up our relationships and devour our self-esteem. The enemy is ultimately trying to take our soul to hell and his intent is not a game. His attempts are not just a "hit" to kill us in this life, but these hits are targeted at our eternity. The hit man against our soul never gives up. He's got our entire lifetime to pursue. However, he is running out of his appointed time however. Not because we are dying, but because his time is dying.

Jesus Christ will come back soon. We may be here for His rapture, or we may already be with Him in death from this life. Nevertheless, the time is closer for Him to return. For this reason, the enemy's strategy starts early in our life. Our children are being exposed and experiencing things we never dreamed of. Teenagers are taking their own lives and the lives of others. Paul told us that these perilous times, the days we currently live in, would come.

For men shall be lovers of their own selves, covetous, boasters, proud, blasphemers, disobedient to parents, unthankful, unholy, without natural affection, trucebreakers, false accusers, incontinent, fierce, despisers of those that are good, traitors, heady, high-minded, lovers of pleasures more than lovers of God.   Having a form of Godliness, but denying the power therefore;

—*2 Timothy 3:2-5*

This is why the enemy's attacks are subtle, distracting, and appear non-threatening. The enemy camouflages himself as an angel of light. He disguises himself in "friendly" people, "pleasant" circumstances, or "attractive" opportunities. The only way to know the difference is to know the one who makes the difference, Jesus. The only way to avoid the pitfalls is to actually listen to who we know and what we know. The Holy Spirit, often referred to as the Christian's sixth sense, exposes the enemy to us. It should be difficult to catch us off guard because we have too much information about the enemy and his tactics. It should be difficult, but unfortunately, we all have blind spots, and as we all know, blind spots can cause severe accidents and even death.

REFLECTIONS

Have we discovered our blind spots? This is not a trick or facetious question. We might arbitrarily answer by stating that if they are blind, we obviously have not discovered them or cannot see them. This is true in most cases, and it continues to be the problem. This is precisely why the enemy's most effective weapon against us is ourselves.

Do we know our vices and we are aware of our weights, you know, the sin that so easily sets us back? Have we learned how to manage our appetites? What lessons have we learned from giving into our vices? Have we put a plan in place to prevent future failures? Have we put significant time and space between us and our vulnerabilities?

Have we replaced our vices with something new and perhaps more destructive? Or, have we developed a strategy against the blind spots in our lives?

If we have not changed what we think about our weights and proclivities, we may have a blind spot to them. Blind spots simply mean that there is an area in our life where our view is obscured. Obscurity is the leading cause of bad decisions because common place and common sense things become hard to grasp due to a lack of focus. Our vision becomes obscured when we are not paying attention to detail. Let me illustrate by disclosing my blind spots that I am working to overcome so that you can be free to admit yours.

Let's start with unmanaged passion and misguided compassion. I am a driver in all aspects of my life. I have tenacity, motivation, and an overwhelming hunger for achievement in my life and the lives of others. As a result of my ambition, I can be impulsive. This is good for accomplishment's sake but not so good if my passion is not managed; meaning put into proper perspective. I am not one that needs a "Getty-up" speech. I am the one that needs the "Woe!" warning. I often have to be reminded to "Have a seat!" I am excited, and from a child I have always looked forward for reasons to remain excited. I think months ahead and toggle the things that I am looking forward to. Even while walking through some of the dark places and seasons in my life, I kept my passion for making plans and having great expectations.

I approach life and make plans with enormous zeal; at home, at work, in relationships, etc. This characteristic is good for encouraging others, but it is not so good if I bulldoze through and as a result, overextend myself. I tend to have a "take it on" attitude about everything I set my heart and mind on and this can cause blind spots. I act impulsively because I have always had a hunger for success, not to compete or to compare myself to anyone, but just to accomplish big goals because I have big dreams. I am not afraid of failing, but I am afraid of running out of time. I feel anxious about not accomplishing everything I hope for and envision. It almost became a problem because I could not figure out how to stop going, climbing, and looking for more to do. I think I hid behind my zeal to escape my hurts, pains, private thoughts or memories of past failures. By acting impulsively, I ignored all the caution signs and repeatedly failed to protect myself, to guard myself, to contemplate and to wait. My attitude was, "I want it and I want it right now because I can make it happen." Perhaps I am over zealous about fulfilling goals and objectives because these are areas I believe I can control, making up for areas I cannot. I cannot control another person's choices. The feeling of abandonment is what I believe drove me to feel like I have to surround myself with accomplishment, or at least surround myself with a list of things to get done so that I am never alone for a long period of time. If I fail to get something done in the timeframe I promised, I negotiate a new deadline and add an additional component to the original goal, even if this process is only done in my head. I am a negotiator by nature. I look for ways to fix it, fix people, or fix situations; and, if I cannot fix it, I find a way to negotiate with people who are depending on me, to make them feel better about it not being fixed...yet.

I am hired for positions and appointed to lead committees for this reason. I am a "do-er," a "see-er," and a "make-er." In fact, my motto in meetings is, "Let's make it happen!" And guess what? We do!

What is so bad about this? It seems great, and everyone watching sees it as great—well not everyone—some see it as frustrating, and others perhaps see it as annoying. What is actually blinding about this? How can vision be blinding?

Unmanaged passion!

Now let's take this passionate energy into my private life, my thoughts, my fears, and yes, my flesh. It is necessary to take ourselves away from the lights and cameras to discover what is truly going on inside and behind the scenes. How did this unmanaged passion affect my self-efficacy? Self-efficacy is one's belief in their ability to succeed in specific situations or to accomplish a task. Our self-efficacy plays a major role in how we perceive ourselves and therefore, how we approach goals, tasks and challenges.

A relentless search for a safe place to land is what I discovered within. After two failed marriages and other heart-wrenching experiences, I was trying to find a safe place for my heart to land. I needed to discover where I could fit in, get comfortable, and position myself to exhale. My heart did not feel safe to rest for a period. Not at home, not with family, and not in the church where I served. I had to come to some "self" realities to trace where I lost my safe place.

In my quest, I discovered that I love to love and to be in love. I long for intimacy. I believe that love-making without conversation is like a beach without sand. Not just the act of sex, but the process of love-making. This was a place that was not safe for my heart because it never found a landing. Intimacy had not been safe. Who was safe seeing in-to-me?

Our generation does not seem to know the essence of love-making and has taken a shortcut and an aimless detour, settling for temporary physical gratification without the benefit of real connection. If people have never seen healthy love demonstrated, they have nothing to gauge from and certainly not much to model after. Television and other warped socialisms provide a perverted depiction of love where there is no discretion, no discernment, and certainly no safety for the heart.

Over the years, I developed a strong heart that can take a punch, a stab, and even a bullet; but this was not, and is not, safe. In spite of assaults, my heart still continues to find its beat and is ready to keep living. My mind is saying that my heart should be dead, or at least in a coma, but it just keeps beating. Thank God for His grace, for I believe that God's grace protects my heart more than I realize. Along with an ever-beating heart comes an appetite for physical connection. An intimate touch is one of the areas that fuels my passion to an unhealthy extent if it is not managed. We have to choose to wait instead of choosing to wonder. If not, we are moving blindly. Sex before or without marital commitment is a blind spot. We live in a society that has lost confidence in marriage with good reason. People go into marriage with a strategy to get out instead of tools and resources to make it work at all costs.

Outside of marriage, if you strive to live celibate to honor your commitment to God and to yourself, there has to be a plan. Failure to plan is planning to fail. If you are celibate for a significant season and fall in a weak moment, you might mistake this for a great sexual experience, sure, but what about soul ties? Pregnancy? STD's? Blind Spots!

Doing first and thinking later is impulsive and can be deceiving. If you go without intimacy long enough, it is easy to fall into sexual relationships, searching to fulfill a natural desire and avoid loneliness. We are human beings and not robots. However, acting on sexual urges without thinking is impulsive and unmanaged passion.

Can we talk openly? Good.

Dating "responsibly and reasonably" is nearly impossible without tools, resources, and guidance, especially for those who have taken the vow of celibacy. Vowing not to engage in sex outside of wedlock is a challenge, especially for an individual who has been married before, who had an active sex life outside of marriage, or someone who has a healthy sexual appetite. However, for those of us who are not married, a vow of celibacy has to be made and committed to, period. Yes, sex outside of marriage is a sin. I know we like to pick and choose what sin is, but it is what *God* says it is. Celibacy can also be a tough issue for spiritual leaders, especially those who are single. Some leaders are in denial and falsely believe that they can float in and out of sexual sin depending upon their next ministry engagement because they are effective with their calling regardless. We do not have a license to take vacations from the truth while teaching it to others. God help us!

But I keep under my body, and bring it into subjection: lest that any means, when I have preached to others, I myself should be a castaway.

—I Corinthians 9:27 (KJV)

In this scripture, Apostle Paul reminds us that people who claim to be spiritual leaders have to make sure that we are living what we teach and preach to others to prevent being condemned by our words. Refusing to make adjustments in our lives to align with God's Word is an example of raising our fists. To act rebelliously against the principles of God is living with raised fists. To compromise the truth by teaching tolerance where

God does not is teaching others to live with raised fists.

The Word we attempt to ascribe to the lives of others has to first reach us, cut us, challenge us, convict us and expose us. This includes the areas of our passion.

The Word of God is alive and powerful. It is sharper than the sharpest sword, cutting between soul and spirit, between joint and marrow. It exposes our innermost thoughts and desires.

—Hebrews 4:12 (NLT)

We need help defining how much is too much and how long is too long. Do we need to define this? When we are single, we need to be honest with ourselves to establish boundaries. We have to determine, for ourselves, how much affection is too much. How much discussion about sex, touching sexually or watching sexual material is too much? On the other hand, how long should we kiss, touch, explore, etc.? That is open for interpretation because it can be applied to both physical and emotional intimacy. *The Wait*, written by Pastor DaVon Franklin and his wife, Megan Good, deals with this very issue. The book is, in my opinion, one of the most compelling and relevant resources for Christians who need guidance on how to begin, change or re-direct behavior concerning unmanaged passion. Relatable to a broad audience, *The Wait* is a change agent that has captured the hearts and minds of both men and women alike. It gives new insight into the subject of unmanaged passion and provides practical tools for Christians who might be struggling with the issue.

Marriage is so much more than a spiritual license to have unsinful sex. Before anything else, married couples should also be friends and have total transparency and trust with one another. In my wait for a safe place for my heart to land, I struggled with the notion that this type of relationship was even possible. From the example witnessed at home, the friends I know who were inflicted with sexual diseases from their spouse, and the failed relationships I survived, there is yet some doubt about this, but I am in pursuit to drop my fists and raise my hands.

People who have been emotionally damaged have a difficult time in marriage because of trust issues. Until an emotionally damaged person overcomes this barrier, no relationship will feel like a safe place for the heart to land regardless of how much time has passed since the initial hurt. Dropping our fists and raising our hands frees the heart and allows us to experience proper healing. I believe the heart repairs much like a bone. Once broken, it has to be set right to heal properly. If it is not set right after a break, it will have to be re-broken and endure the re-setting process for it to heal properly. How is the heart "set right" after a break? By allowing the break to hurt and then allowing the break to heal. Many people do not even want to acknowledge the break much less feel its pain. Let's review the broken bone again.

When a bone is broken, it is damaged for a season, it may bleed internally, it may swell, and it may be sore for awhile; but in time, if it is correctly set back in place, wrapped up to avoid injury, and released from tension, it will fully heal. The healing of a broken heart is similar. When our heart is broken, it is damaged and may bleed internally, meaning that it will have some deep wounds that have to heal from the inside out. This may feel heavy on our chest, like a lump in our throat, not to mention the weight it carries on our mind. It may be that no position relieves the pain for a while, but if we raise our hands, we allow God to wrap and protect our hearts to avoid more injury. Our job is to be still while it heals. This is not easy because we generally want our heart to heal faster than it actually will. We invest in long-term commitments and then want quick healing if the commitment ends. If the relationship took ten years to build, it won't heal in ten days or perhaps even ten months if it dissolves. People often self-medicate when their heart breaks. Trauma is an uncontrollable feeling, so people seek a quick comfort from the pain. Unfortunately, this causes more injury, delays the healing process and can produce addictions.

There are many people who live together faithfully in marriage for a lifetime as best friends, lovers, partners, ride or die, or what have you; when you look your worst, smell your worst, and act your worst, that partner's love is still unconditional. But what happens when your partner is incapacitated and cannot perform physically? You are still best friends and lovers because your commitment is much deeper than the surface stuff. This is the principle that seems to get lost, diminished, or rejected today. People enter into commitment with three exit doors. Great sexual experiences shared between a committed couple are not intended to have the same euphoric effect as drugs where there is always a strive to find your initial high. In marriage, love-making and the sexual experience should be a consistent high because you have committed a lifetime to discovering how to make it your first time every time. Where is this being taught, sought, and thought? Where is it safe to love and to be loved? Where is it safe to land?

All that being said and understood now, over the past three decades, a safe place to land is what I was longing for while raising two daughters, leading several ministries and managing priorities, programs, and people.

My Salve left before my daughter's first birthday, leaving a diaper and ten dollar bill in my mailbox. When I was going through the grueling process of obtaining financial support for my baby, I encountered my Blind Spot. Ironically, I met my Blind Spot on a blind date. In hindsight, I am not sure that going into anything blind is wise. Too much blindness can cause a major collision. We talked on the phone for long hours a few days before. When we met for the first time, my heart, my mind—all of my senses leaped, awakened and became totally engaged. There was an immediate chemistry between us, and he asked me to be his exclusively very quickly. I did my due diligence of conducting a character reference check with credible sources. The initial feedback was in alignment with his disclosures. My unmanaged passion became an untamed lioness. I quickly found myself vulnerable to my blind spot because my emotions had completely dulled my spiritual senses. Over time, when I could hear God again, I began to discern that this new relationship was driving broad side in my emotional blind spot, meaning that I could sense he was hiding something and withholding details when he volunteered confessions from his past. There were issues of the heart that seemed hidden and non-disclosed, like holes in his stories about his upbringing, or his sarcasm when asked to elaborate on details that were purposely left out of the information he shared. Unmanaged passion often leads to misguided compassion because we lose our frame of reference and become less spiritually coherent.

Misguided compassion is the inability to call a spade a spade because we cannot see clearly with our emotions, our clouded thoughts and aroused flesh in the way. We quickly forget that if someone or something does not feel right, it is most likely not right. To paraphrase Maya Angelou, "The first time a person shows you who they are, believe them." This is not a judgmental or negative view; it is safe. Misguided compassion happens when we attempt to see things the way we wish they were and miss what they actually are. We dismiss signs and second guess our gut notions.

I dismissed My Blind Spot's issues as struggles he was too ashamed to deal with. I put on my ministry lens and therefore did not guard my heart. We cannot put on a ministry hat after we failed to put on discernment and expect to see without bias. The doctor and the patient are subject to the same ailments; however, the doctor cannot objectively work on the patient if he/she is emotionally connected to them. We should probably avoid dating our patients or students because aside from being morally taboo, there might be a conflict of interest. The same is true in ministry. Separation of spiritual-overdrive and carnal overdrive is necessary because if we allow the two to collide, we miss blind spots. Spiritual-overdrive is when we believe that we are stronger spiritually than we really are. When I met my Blind Spot, I was leading several ministries: a college campus organization, a community at-risk youth program, developing a non-profit ministry, and then asked to oversee a church where women do not pastor. That is spiritual overdrive. Too many distractions to pay attention. Just because it is spiritual does not make it appropriate if it causes us not to see what is in front of us or to ignore what is obvious.

My Blind Spot did not seem ashamed of his actions, only ashamed of getting exposed. His ego and his issues were real, and they hung from him as bright as ornaments on a Christmas tree; however, they seemed camouflaged in the midst of his church and place of employment.

There were red flags, purple flags, and orange flags, all of them easily recognizable, but I ignored them just the same. My Blind Spot became a permanent fixture in my vision; I just adjusted my mirrors to accommodate. I failed to look over my shoulder to see what was really there. This relationship took its toll for over a decade. Blinds spots waste time, exhaust hearts and confuse the mind.

You see, we can operate in all facets of life with a blind spot. We can even move the object in and out of our blind areas, but until we are willing to totally detach, take a sharp turn, or stop and let it pass, we will engage in a terrible Risk Agreement and spend time and energy on the wrong thing for a long time.

Risk Agreements and the conclusion of my Blind Spot experience are discussed in Chapter 3. In the meantime, if you have a blind spot, you have raised fists. The way to get rid of the blind spot is to expose it. It is broadside, so move it into clear view. Shoot, run it over, then back up and run over it again. Bring it out of hiding and don't allow it to linger out of site while still connected to you. If you do, it might cause you to get into a terrible accident that could very well be fatal.

The Strategy of the Hit List

Often times, the enemy does not *charge* at you; he seduces you with your own desires. Like the blind spot, the enemy may initially attempt to be a charming friend or lover, just fitting right in so they can get in. He uses decoys that initially seem benign (to lower our defenses), but this type of trickery only exploits our weaknesses to keep us bound: false intimacy, alcohol and drug abuse, and toxic relationships. All subtleties that seem harmless at first because of the way they make us *feel*, but beneath the surface, they are actually lethal. By the time the truth is exposed, we are faced with life-changing consequences: divorce, fired from work, a child in trouble, an unfaithful spouse, and deception in our own mind. This is all the strategy of the enemy's Hit List!

Once we allow the enemy leverage, he has our ear and will suggest things to take us out and under. His goal is for us to be invested, locked in, and sold out so that when he exposes his hand, we will feel trapped and stuck. Staying *in* seems more sensible because getting out is too arduous.

We have protection. God has a bulletproof hedge that doesn't just protect us from the front, but it is like a fence all around us. God's bullet-proof hedges are the angels that are encamped around about us, the mercy and grace that follow us, and the shadow of the Almighty that covers us. He is our way out of every entrapment. He is our protection from and our deliverance out of our Blind Spots. It does not matter how far in we may think we are, God can deliver us out of it ALL.

The angel of the Lord encampeth round about them that fear him, and delivereth them.

—Psalm 34:7

Is there anything we can do to fight back without using raised fists? Yes, there is something we can do. *Drop our fists and raise our hands*. This is the action of putting down our limited emotional weaponry and raising our hands in complete and total surrender to God. This is the spiritual response to the spiritual battle. That's right! The way out is down and then *up*. Drop your fists and raise your hands. This is a new weapon to add to your arsenal against the enemy.

"When the wicked enemy, even mine enemies and my foes, came upon me to eat up my flesh they stumbled and fell."

I like this part best.

"Though an host should encamp against me, my heart shall not fear; though war should rise against me, in this will I be confident"

—Psalm 27:2-3

David's confidence was in knowing that he was on the right track even while on the Hit List. The greater the threat you pose, the bigger your challenge. Dropping our fists and raising our hands is a dichotomy that is hard to embrace. Being quiet amid a trying time can be difficult. Practicing self-discipline while being under the enemy's attack requires a new mindset. Dropping our fists and raising our hands is a paradigm shift. This concept is not a casual or laissez-faire response to a fight. It is an aggressive stance because we are putting God in front of us while we hide in Him. To many, this may sound like a hard, and even strange concept to grasp, but it is necessary and effective, especially in battle.

Multiple Hits

Have you ever been through more than one difficult situation happening at one time, or experienced recurring situations? Have you ever felt like requesting a new trial? Multiple hits can be overwhelming.

Take debt for example. "God, I'm tired of scraping from one paycheck to the next. I'm worn out worrying how I am going to make ends meet. Can I get the flu instead?" At least with the flu, we know the prognosis of the condition. We even know what symptoms to expect. We may get a fever, experience some painful aches. It may even become difficult to swallow, breathe clearly and taste food, but we know once we take the prescribed medication, the sickness will pass within 7 to 10 days.

Do you ever feel like asking God to give you something that won't take forever to get rid of?

Let me not have to deal with that difficult situation or person for just one week. Make my husband treat me like I should be treated. Stop folks from lying, cheating, and trying to manipulate me. Lord, why do I have to see so much hatred in the church? Lord, why do I have to stay here and deal with this mess? I can only take so much. I'm tired of being alone and lonely. I'm sick of trying every diet and every exercise and never losing any weight. Can we please move onto something else, God?

What is God trying to get out of us with heaviness? What are we to take away from the situation? *Nothing.* We are to take nothing away, but instead, make additions to our character, our discipline, and our faith.

"...add to your faith goodness, and to goodness, knowledge; and to knowledge, self-control; and to self-control, perseverance; and to perseverance, godliness; and to godliness, mutual affection; and to mutual affection, love."

—2 Peter 1:5-7

Experiencing multiple hits might get heavy, but I have learned that when the battle gets the heaviest is when I am about to experience the biggest breakthrough. I have yet to discover why that is. Perhaps it is because I am more ready to receive. Perhaps my heart is more pliable. When Jesus told us not to be surprised if the world hates us, He must have been speaking of the church world too. In fact, that may be the world He was exclusively referring to. Church hurt is the worst type of pain because this is where we escape from our trouble, right? Well, let's not be too hasty and think we can trust all people. Remember, church people are just like anybody else, subject to the elements that cause raised fists. From the pulpit to the door, people need to drop their fists and raise their hands.

As God is shifting us and transitioning us for new levels of understanding and empowerment, we will encounter *chaff* and *tares*.

The Chaff

Chaff is defined as worthless things or trash; as such, I am not surprised that Chaff is a major weapon the enemy uses to hit us right in the center of who we are. In the Bible, Chaff is used to define ungodly people, wicked people, or wickedness.

The ungodly are not so: but are like the chaff which the wind driveth away. Therefore, the ungodly shall not stand in the judgment, nor sinners in the congregation of the righteous. For the Lord knoweth the way of the righteous: but the way of the ungodly (chaff) shall perish.

—Psalm 1: 4-6

Chaff is an antagonistic force that operates within people to mock others. Chaff is not subtle in its approach to exploit our struggles, our bad habits, and our vulnerabilities because the intent is to derail our influence and attack the perception of our integrity. Chaff is like a roaring lion waiting for an opportunity to pounce on you and then finish you off once you fall. Chaff is the noise that competes with your inner voice to suggest that you will never be taken seriously, that you are irrelevant, and that no one cares about you. Chaff is the enemy's strategic partner that studies you and then lays in wait to destroy you, especially when you already feel defeated, discouraged, lonely, confused, and desperate. Chaff is responsible for many suicides and homicides. It is also one of the leading causes of various types of addictions.

How is Chaff even able to reach us and do so much potential damage?

Chaff is cultivated by the enemy and speaks directly to your mind with no compassion or shame. The enemy cunningly gets into people of influence, specifically those with direct influence upon your life, to ensure chaff doesn't miss the Hit. If the hit it not successful in taking us out or leaving us crippled emotionally, chaff will multiply itself to reach the ears of more people and put dirt in their minds about you. With this broadened base of hate, conspiracies and public attacks on your character will abound, ruining your reputation with others. All the while, chaff is just an internal noise that causes external chaos by infiltrating our mindsets and causing us to do wicked things. Chaff is the master of discord. It will bypass people of little concern or consequence to you (like Chatty, Messy, and Busybody), and move right into your leader, your teacher, manager, spouse, friend, etc.

Chaff premeditates our demise with a scheme to set us up. Have you ever been set up by someone that should have had your back? Have you ever experienced a conspiracy that had your name at the top of the file? This can cause us to immediately raise up our emotional and actual fists (and it often does). That is our natural tendency, but we are going to discover how to change our natural tendencies in response to Chaff.

Now, the good news is that Chaff is actually working for your good because we are typically challenged by where we are going and not where we left. Chaff provides an indication that a move is about to take place in our life. Chaff will have people attack your character and they won't even know why they are doing it.

The Biblical character Daniel determined that he would not partake in the king's favor by eating the king's special diets and delicacies. As soon as Daniel and his three friends took this stand, the enemy started to conspire against them. The three friends (Shadrack, Meshach, and Abednego), were thrown into a fiery furnace where God saved them. Daniel was also saved, but in the Lion's Den. They applied the principle of *Drop Your Fists and Raise Your Hands*. When we use this principle, we allow *God* an opportunity to show Himself strong on our behalf, because clearly there will be circumstances that we cannot conquer alone.

What happened to the conspirators? They were discarded as *trash*. Some were even thrown into the furnace while others were fed to the lions. That is the purpose of Chaff in our lives. God uses it to test our faith, and once we prove ourselves, Chaff is destroyed, discarded, and tossed into the pit that was intended for you. We, however, are blessed with a new dimension of strength, might, and opportunity. This reason alone is good enough to learn the principle of Drop Your Fists and Raise Your Hands.

Chaff teaches us that every offer is not an opportunity, every smile is not sincere, and every handshake is not a promise. We learn these lessons from Chaff as we experience people who deliberately try to make us fail by lying, withholding information, attempting to publicly humiliate, or who stir up discord behind the scenes. Further, every connection is not connected to you, while everything that connects to you is not a sincere connection. My Blind Spot taught me that. People will try to connect to you because your influence can benefit them. It is unfortunate that people will actually use your love for them *against* you. Why? Because you are on the Hit List!

Jesus taught us that everyone you minister to and everyone who is blessed by your anointing might not even like you or respect you. In fact, they are sometimes the very ones in Chaff's grandstand precluding judgment of the very hell that made your anointing so powerful in their lives. Chaff is crass and cruel. As soon as you recognize this characteristic in someone, walk away.

Chaff will subtly have you stray away from your loved ones until you end up alone. The easiest way to take you out is when you are seemingly by yourself because then you are a clear shot. That's why the first thing the enemy brings to your mind in the midst of adversity is to escape. He will attempt to engage your mind, having you looking at everyone crossed-eyed and with a raised eyebrow.

Straying from your family and friends isn't the only consequence of Chaff. It can also cause you to think negatively about the people in your life. You will hear whispers: "I just don't understand why he's with her," "I just can't see why he's on his second marriage and trying to preach, "or, "I can't receive her ministry."

CHAFF!

But God has something for the Chaff in Isaiah 5.

Therefore, as the fire devoureth the stubble, and the flame consumeth the chaff, so their root shall be as rottenness, and their blossom shall go up as dust..."

We also have to be careful that *we* do not become Chaff. This behavior can easily make its home in our hearts just as it does in the enemy's heart. If we do not recognize the enemy's blows, negativisms, opposition, and ignorance as Chaff and instead internalize the Hit, we can begin to become Chaff ourselves. If self-righteousness starts to take root in our hearts, our fists will go right up. We may begin to have an attitude that nobody is saved but us. Humph, and if they're saved, they aren't filled with the Spirit. You will begin to isolate yourself from everyone and everything, believing that you are practicing sanctification.

And if this happens, guess what? *You* have just become *Chaff*. The downward spiral of Chaff will cause you to become delusional. Your behavior might even mimic most (if not all) of the following list:

- You haven't picked up your Bible between church service and Bible Study, but you are more sanctified and saved than the person who is annoying you.

- You haven't set aside a specific time to commune with God like you once did because you are upset, but you are still better than your pew partners.

- You have an unresolved issue with your sister or your brother, but rather than come clean and deal with the issue, you go under and out in the spirit.

- Oh, and let's not forget the best one: people speaking in an unknown tongue cannot seem to speak the common language needed to bring unity and restoration. CHAFF!

Self-righteousness is a pompous attitude that is often undetected because, once we have been illuminated to the truth of God's Word, we can lose a sense of compassion trying to be *right*. People can quickly become overly critical of others when they are guilty themselves. Even more so, people are critical of others in areas they perceive *themselves* not to struggle in. For example, if I do not have a proclivity toward drugs, that is where I hang my hat when I am teaching and preaching. But, I am less vocal in the "Amen" section when someone is teaching about an issue I have not overcome. This is hypocrisy. It is hypocritical to secretly partake in a sin then rebuke others who are struggling with the same thing. It is hypocritical to condemn someone for an activity that *God* does not condemn them for, such as drinking wine, dancing, wearing certain articles of clothing, listening to various genres of music, wearing makeup, etc. We are accountable to lead others to *God's* righteousness and not our *own* ideologies. We fall into the trap of self-righteousness when we attempt to counter-transfer our issues, experiences, dislikes, etc., on to someone else without any Biblical base or support. Chaff!

The most important attribute of chaff is that it is TRASH and easily disposable. Recognize it, separate it from value, put it in a bag, and toss it. Or better yet, burnt it.

The Tares

The enemy plants TARES in the Body of Christ, in our homes, in our churches, at our jobs, and among our close friends and associates. Unlike Chaff, which is an inside enemy, *tares* are external: individuals or a group of individuals used by the enemy to sew discord, confusion, and strife.

The Kingdom of Heaven is like a man who sowed good seed in his field; but while he slept, his enemy came and sowed tares among the wheat and went his way.

—Matthew 13:24-25

The enemy has a strategy to discredit our goodness; as frail, finite and fragile as our attempt to be "good" is, to dismantle us. The enemy targets who *we* value and who values us. That is his "bull's-eye" in our lives. He attempts to unravel and unsettle our relationships with misunderstandings, miscommunications, confusion, jealousy, conspiracy, lies, and hurtful truths. Tares tend to materialize among the important people in our lives, which is why they are able to camouflage themselves among the good wheat (normalcies) in our lives.

No one is exempt from tares. Let's explore some examples.

A spouse who lives a double life is a *tare* planted right in your intimate and safe place. Long before a *tare* is exposed, the deceit is deeply embedded in their heart and in their mind. A *tare* has planned out their deviant behavior long before you are victimized by it. Unfaithfulness often happens in the heart long before it is exposed. This is why the blow can be so devastating and at first, unbelievable. Infidelity involves time, effort, and

131

premeditated coordination. People can be married for a long time before they find out that tares have been growing among the wheat of their home. As we know, adultery is a breach of the marriage covenant and manifests in many ways: physical contact, emotional contact, forgery, embezzlement, and perversions. What we often fail to discuss is that infidelity is a *choice*. One chooses to dismiss their commitment made to God, to their spouse, and in the presence of others when they cheat. He does not fall into her; I mean the act. She is not raped by him; I mean the notion. It is a *choice* to raise our fists and to cheat on our way out of a legal and spiritual contract, and there is no excuse or reason that validates the behavior. Let's put this out there to help someone deal with this issue openly. It is not natural, a spontaneous act or a mistake. It is a choice.

Tares can live and breed among your life without you even noticing them. By the time you become aware of them, it might be too late to do anything about it. It is a hot mess, to say the least, and to discover you are right in the middle of the field with both wheat and tares is a revelation that some simply cannot handle. This vile reality is the number one cause of failed marriages, breaking up homes and causing financial devastation.

...who winks maliciously with his eye, signals with his feet and motions with his fingers, who plots evil with deceit in his heart—he always stirs up conflict.

Therefore, disaster will overtake him in an instant;
he will suddenly be destroyed-without remedy.

—Proverbs 6:13-15

God knows our thoughts afar off. He knows and judges the intent of the heart. Some people are deceived into believing that nobody knows their "real" intentions or how they *really* feel or what they *truly* mean. God is *all* knowing and thank goodness He is also *all* protecting. Just take a moment to think of what God did *not* allow to happen. Although it will not feel like it at the time, a person's unfaithfulness could very well be God *terminating* them from your life. God can and often does terminate people while they are still in position, wilding out, showing out, and flossing. For example, God had fired King Saul while he was still in position and while he sent Prophet Samuel to Jesse's house to anoint David as the next King. Saul still lived in the palace, gave out orders, and operated as the iconic public leader, but he was divinely terminated. By the time a Tare in your life knows anything, their key no longer works to your house or your heart; their office is cleaned out, their name is removed from the title, or they have simply been replaced. Divine termination!

The Lord said to Samuel, "How long will you mourn
for Saul, since I have rejected him as king over
Israel? Fill your horn with oil and be on your way; I

am sending you to Jesse of Bethlehem. I have chosen one of his sons to be king."

—I Samuel 16:1

Without the indwelling of the Holy Spirit, it is becoming more difficult to know the real from the rally. It is not a new phenomenon. How did we become so undiscerning that the enemy is able to create so much mayhem right in our midst and we miss it? How did this happen?

In relationships, it is because we chose to take the risk to love. Allowing ourselves to become intimate with another person involves taking a risk and allowing ourselves to be vulnerable. When we first feel the flutters of love, we are more vulnerable than we realize or even want to admit. This is a good place for the enemy to sow tares. If we choose to get involved with a person who has a history of cheating in relationships, this may be a *tare*. Or, if we move beyond the "honeymoon phase" and really get to know a person and develop a level of trust and admiration beyond butterflies and infatuation, this is also a good place for the enemy to sow tares. Now, once we share our hearts, thoughts, and perhaps our body with a person, this is the *ultimate* place for the enemy to sow tares. If you are attempting to start a relationship with someone while they are experiencing marital failure, this is a good place for the enemy to sow a tare in your life.

Essentially, *any* time is the enemy's opportune time to tear with a *tare*. We are human, subject to feel, subject to love, and therefore, subject to be torn by tares. This happens in other areas of life, not just our romantic relationships.

We are caught off guard when the people who are closest to us turn out to be our fatal enemy. We are devastated when we discover that someone we shared our heart with, expressed anguish to, laughed with, and cried with revealed our innermost thoughts to someone else. *Tares*!

For it was not an enemy that reproached (deceived) me; then I could have borne it (taken it better): neither was it he that hated me that did magnify himself against me; then I would have hidden myself from him (prevented it)

But it was thou, a man mine equal, my guide, and mine acquaintance.

We took sweet counsel together, and walked unto the house of God in company.

—Psalm 55: 12-14 (KJV)

When you have the emotional wind knocked out of you by a tare's attack, you may begin to raise your fists from the hurt and frustration. Over time; however, if issues are not resolved in our hearts, we may not drop our fists, and this condition can become bondage. Bondage on a person's heart is heavy and can last for many years. Bondage is hard to live with, but sometimes harder to let go of. Letting go is the only way to freedom.

We have talked about the subtlety of planted tares, but now let's take a look at the grown tares among the wheat. Remember, tares are part of the center or core of your associations: your family, co-worker, church member, or team member. Tares grow with you, eat with you, see you often, share with you, and for this reason, you believe you know them. They are close. Let's look at an example of grown tares from a story in the Bible.

The city and everything that is in it shall be under the ban (designated to be destroyed in as a form of tribute) to the Lord...

But Achan (Tare) took some of the things under the ban and the Lord's anger burned against Israel.

—Joshua 6-8

Like Achan behaved among Israel, *tares* often exhibit behavior that is questionable, inappropriate, or insubordinate. They are usually the person in the group who stirs up mess, causes confusion, and sews discord; however, they may not appear treacherous or malignant. These are the people who just blend in for the purpose of tearing things up from the inside out. They are typically insecure with low self-esteem and passive-aggressive tendencies. We see them, but we do not recognize their venom because they seem to be genuine. We believe they are showing their hands, so why second guess their hearts?

The same is true for people who steal and cheat. Theft typically happens at night when the owners are sleeping, and unfaithful sexting, instant messaging, private video chatting, and other forms of unfaithful communications are done after dark as well. Tares are sown by careless people while responsible people are asleep.

This is not just behavior typical of non-church folk; people in the church have fallen away from having a healthy fear of God, and as a result, they can sow just as many Tares as non-church goers. Where there is no fear of God, there is confusion, lack of direction, and the impossibility of making sound decisions. This is simply because the "fear of God" is the beginning of wisdom.

The antonym for wisdom is foolishness. When we begin to witness a lot of foolishness and deal with foolish people, we are really dealing with a person who is void of understanding, and sagacity. We are dealing with *tares*. The adversary doesn't just attempt to trip us up with negativity, he comes subtly, with peace appeal, often camouflaging his real intent. This is why he uses people and circumstances that are up close and personal to us. We are less likely, so he (the enemy) thinks, to recognize him. We are in warfare, but we often find ourselves fighting the wrong battle or fighting the intended battle the wrong way. Let's equip ourselves with the principle of *Drop Your Fists and Raise Your Hands*.

CHAPTER BREAK

CHAPTER 3
"DROP EM"

Surrendering the will has always been the most challenging battle because our flesh will never willingly surrender, but will always desire to gratify and justify. The phrase or term "the flesh" refers to the *essence* of who we are and not just our physical body. The flesh refers to that part of us that is alienated from God; the rebellious, unruly, and obstinate part of our inner-self that must *choose* to surrender to God. The flesh is the part that does not want to be told what to do. For the context of this chapter, we will work under this denotation.

The mind governed by the flesh is hostile to God; it does not submit to God's law, nor can it do so.

—Romans 8:7 (NIV)

For many reasons, people simply do not freely give up their will to God. Most of us have to go through a life-enlightening or a life-threatening experience before we finally surrender our lives to

God. If we as adults treat God like a "Genie in a Bottle," expecting Him to grant our every wish without any level of responsibility, how can we expect our children not to live with a sense of entitlement?

It is good to make opportunities accessible, but it is not wise to enable, coddle, and handhold excessively. Children should be taught how to do some things for *themselves* and experience the consequences of not making good decisions. Yes, living with a sense of entitlement cripples people because it creates an expectation to receive without properly understanding how to ask for something; believing that it is *owed* to you. It also diminishes a person's willingness to work for what they need and desire. "Please" and "Thank you," have turned into "Now" and a disrespectful "head nod." We have failed to chastise our children or give them consequences for negative behavior, and as a result, they enter into adulthood expecting the same treatment from the world. And as we are experiencing, the disparities and injustices within the "system" exacerbate this perilous mindset.

We need to instill in this generation the value of hard work and teach them refinement and self-control by exhibiting these traits in our own behavior. America has declined in education and increased incarcerations, predominately among this generation. Young people are not being disciplined to respect their parent's authority and therefore become a liability to our communities and a risk to employ because they lack respect. Social Media is a primary source of entertainment, information, and social interaction and seems to have replaced family bonding time. Families have lost the sense of closeness through intimate communication because everybody around the dinner table has their cell phone out. Not in every home, but in a lot. Just observe people at restaurants. How many couples are actually talking? Are kids being engaged? Or, are they being ignored and left to entertain themselves? Where are we learning etiquette, professionalism, or how to properly address authority?

Fornication, adultery, and pornography have become "normal" in our society. The lack of family bonding leads to children not knowing how to conduct themselves. Intimate scenes in film involve people younger than 25. Youth-oriented shows depict immature young people experiencing intimate behavior without adult guidance or involvement. As a result, our young people between the ages of 10 and 17 are being enticed to make adult decisions when they are not emotionally mature enough to handle the consequences that can and often do occur.

It is imperative that we reach our coming generations and instill in them the principles of obedience, humility, patience, and surrender. They need to be taught spiritual and practical values that will equip them to take a stand against the world's frolicking temptations.

It used to be that church kids had the worst reputation and experienced more problems with promiscuity, addiction, and incarceration. Now, they are no longer singled out because they just blend in. There seems to be no differentiation between kids raised in the church and those who are not. The family nucleus in our churches is under tremendous satanic attack and wholesomeness is becoming extinct. More and more youth are becoming victims of divorce, abuse, neglect, perversion, addiction, and rejection from their parents, teachers, peers, etc. The church, once designed to be a safe haven (and specifically organized to safely nurture and mature young people in the ways of God), has been spiraling downward for decades all the while chasing fame and fortune.

In an era where everybody is fighting to push political and perverse agendas, we have to teach our kids how to drop their fists, emotional and otherwise, by our precept, our transparency, and our example. We have to illustrate that dropping our fists liberates us from excuses, complacency, inability, and insecurity. You see, to hold up raised fists is to hold on to hurt and to remain incarcerated by the associated pain. Over time, holding up raised fists is extremely heavy, laborious, and exhausting.

Clearly, our children are mimicking our behavior, and until we learn to drop our fists, we will always be poor examples for them. But, in order for us to discover how to be better examples, I think we need to delve deeper into why so many of us are walking around with raised fists as opposed to actually engaging in contact. Raised fists without an exchange is just holding an awkward position just in case something happens. People are in this position because something has already happened in the past or because something has threatened to happen, but we only need to raise our fists to first block a blow and then to strike back. The fighting stance indicates an expectation of confrontation and is not a gesture of surrendering all and waiting for change. Dropping our fists indicates that we are not intimidated by an empty threat, focused on a past threat, or afraid of an oncoming threat.

For God has not given us the spirit of fear and timidity, but of power, love and self-discipline.

—2 Timothy 1:7 (NLT)

God has equipped us to respond to obstacles with power, His love and self-control. Dropping our fists and raising our hands is empowering and allows love to flow from our hearts to others.

COMMERCIAL BREAK

Like a lot of people, I have been exposed to many potential threats of "what *may* happen," but I have learned to refuse to wait around, pacing in torment while waiting for what may never take place. And, when terrible things did happen, I battled those memories for years until I finally made the decision to stop letting them control me. I have learned to intentionally say to myself, "Drop em!"

When the enemy tries to intimidate me with haters who criticize, judge, whisper, find fault or attempt to "come for me," so to speak, I say to myself, "Drop em!" This keeps them at bay and also keeps me from having to "grab and pin" them prematurely.

One of the crucial lessons I teach in college ministry are the Rules of Engagement. Some people are good managers but poor leaders or employees simply because they lack interpersonal skills. Some of the brightest and hopeful employees remain stagnant and non-eligible to promote because they cannot collaborate (work well with others).

Rules of Engagement deals with interpersonal interactions. The college ministry I shepherded for eight years was an on-campus organization that started out as a weekly bible study and eventually grew into a ministry. The participants were students from a broad spectrum of diversity: some were raised in an inner-city, some in foster care, some from broken homes, some from abusive and violent environments, some from affluent means, and others were career-bound students who were raised in the church but had fallen away from it. Some students were simply curious about the Gospel. They were open, attentive, consistent, real, intelligent, and hungry for God. Their pliable hearts were a true minister's dream. Teaching the fundamental concepts of how to interact with people was beneficial for this diverse group of young people. College is the season in life when we are exposed to multi-faceted people; different cultures, races, ethnicities and personalities. Leaning how to work with others is essential.

The wisest man said to have ever lived was King Solomon. He obtained his divine wisdom by admitting his insufficiencies and by asking God to teach him the Rules of Engagement.

"···But I am only a child and do not know how to carry out my duties. Your servant is here among the people you have chosen, a great people, too numerous to count or number. So give your servant

a discerning heart to govern your people and to distinguish between right and wrong.

—*I Kings 3:7-9 (NIV)*

King Solomon was wise enough to humble himself to ask for "help" to deal with people. And today, we should do the same thing — ask God to help us get along with people in order to learn to reciprocate learning, respect, and growth. We will encounter difficult people. We may have to respond to awkward situations, and, it is necessary to find out how to "go in and out" among all types of people.

We must teach people the Rules of Engagement to help them obtain employment, get promoted, and effectively deal with bullies. There has been increased awareness of bullying in schools, the corporate world, and in the church. There is an appropriate way to get a bully off of you, professionally, personally and spiritually, even within the principle of drop your fists. I call the term, "grab and pin." This is the quick process of *cutting* a person's attempt to hurt you without cruelty or being indignant or indecent. How do we do that? By succinctly responding with an obvious truth. This is notable because this is also the same way to get the enemy off of you—with an obvious truth. Jesus asked the church bullies this question.

"Why do you look at the speck of sawdust in your brother's eye and pay no attention to the plank in your own eye?"

—Matthew 7:3

The question was brief, to the point, and true. While leading the college ministry, I often emphasized that we do not have to become "ignant" (ignorant) every time we are confronted. "Ignant" is urban slang used to describe how we can react at times when people are rude and obnoxious toward us before we have an opportunity to put on the whole armor of God. It implies that we know how to act but *chose* to act foolishly anyway. It does not promote the principle of drop your fists because it can actually become the preamble to a verbal or physical fight. Ministering to many from the inner-city, I learned just how quickly verbal and physical altercations could occur. Thankfully, the ministry students who were from the inner city were eager to learn a better way to handle conflict and confrontation.

I encountered multiple battles when I started this book: with my family, church members, my child's father, employees at work, and my health. Eight years after having my first child, I became pregnant with my baby girl and once again struggled with a dangerous bout of preeclampsia and gestational diabetes. I had to shorten the phrase "drop your fists" to something quick and powerful, "Drop em!" This two-word method saved me from many unnecessary and meaningless altercations. It is still working for me today.

When the enemy attempts to set the image reel of past painful situations in motion, I say within, "Drop em!" Our minds are so elaborately created that we are capable of total recall of a painful memory to the degree that the details are vivid and the emotions are fresh. The enemy uses these images to distract us and to dismantle our peace.

When I feel uncertain or afraid to take risks, I have learned to say, "Drop em!" If we are not willing to take risks, we will forfeit opportunities. The enemy tries to keep us intimidated by what we perceive as a lack of ability. He can cause doubt, dismay, and discouragement if we allow him to.

Even while I am writing this book with the enemy telling me that it is too late, too transparent, that I am too old and that it will not be successful, I am yet saying, "Drop em!"

The battle may continue, but the way we respond will not. The enemy will try to position us as Easy Prey, but we will refuse to be coiled into mental, emotional or spiritual traps.

How we respond in battle is a matter of heart and will. Dropping our fists is not something that will just happen *for* us. It will also not just "occur" as time passes; it will only become a principle in our lives with practice. How then, do we drop our fists?

We deal with truth. The best way to start the practice and the process is by taking inventory.

Exercise 3, Personal Inventory, is a great place to begin the process of dropping our fists. This personal inventory exercise will explore the triggers, people, places, or events that have left scars in our lives.

Negative feelings are not comfortable, they are heavy in our hearts, and they are weights on our minds. We want out! We want closure!

EXERCISE #3
PERSONAL INVENTORY

Let's take the time to personally inventory the past, perceived or present issues that cause us to raise our emotional fists. Once we complete the inventory, we will begin to peel the layers back, intentionally and deliberately, of each situation, obstacle, hurt, pain or challenge.

Several inventory lists have been started below that will allow us to examine the areas in our life where we may have raised fists. It is important for us to look deep within ourselves to see what we perceive as *threats* to our life. A *threat* in this context is anything that we worry about because we believe that it may bring harm to our lives; naturally and spiritually.

For this exercise, we will identify *painful memories* that we cannot let go of in order to live *liberated* from our past.

We will also identify things we worry about in order to make a choice to drop our fists and let the emotional bondage go to raise our hands and heal.

It is important to forgive *ourselves*. We may have gone through an experience where our choices or actions negatively impacted someone else, and we have things that we regret. God forgives, but people never forget; so, in between grace and condemnation, we have to drop our fists and raise our hands to liberate ourselves from guilt and shame.

Lastly, *fear* can cause us to live a life of raised fists. Confronting our fear allows us to drop our fists and instead surrender this area to God with raised hands.

This exercise has three parts: a) identify, b) give it to God, and c) let it go.

PART I: IDENTIFY

1) Read the categories. Add to the lists with your personal reflections in the blank spaces (You may need to put overflow remarks in the Drop Your Fists 21-Day Journal).

Note: Get it *all* written out and do not hold anything in or back. This is *your* inventory list. No one will see it and no one will judge you for it.

   I. Painful Memories
       1. He or She left me
       2. No one protected me
       3. _____

4. _____
5. _____

II. Things I worry about
   1. I may get hurt again
   2. I may lose this opportunity
   3. _____
   4. _____
   5. _____

III. My Regrets
   1. My addiction destroyed my family
   2. I was selfish and lost everything
   3. _____
   4. _____
   5. _____

IV. Things that I am fearful of
   1. What if it does not work
   2. I am running out of time
   3. _____
   4. _____
   5. _____

I am sure many of you are coming to this journey from many different walks of life, but no matter how varied the answers to this exercise might be, one thing is for certain: there is a vast list of real threats, issues, situations, emotions and perceptions that the enemy uses to draw us into his lair of lies in order to condition us to live with fear, anger, bitterness or emotional dormancy.

PART II: GIVE IT TO GOD

Now, we are going to follow the example of Hezekiah in Isaiah 37. A little background to Hezekiah's story is that he was constantly being threatened by a bully—a king who ordered a succinct Hit on several nations and carried it out successfully. He threatened Hezekiah on several occasions, pointing out his successful history of taking nations out, to the extent that he formally sent Hezekiah a letter outlining his intent to destroy him. The letter also boasted that God would not be able to stop him.

Considering Hezekiah's story, let's continue our exercise. The next step is divided into three parts:

1) Read the Inventory list aloud to yourself.
2) Spread the Inventory out before the Lord.
3) Model the prayer of Hezekiah before the Lord. You are going to pray and ask God for four specific things while laying out the circumstance plainly. Hezekiah was worn out by the king's threats. He may have been intimidated too. He took a courageous step in faith to conquer his fear and to stop the screams of the enemy. He found a quiet place, read the letter and then spread it out before

the Lord. Then, Hezekiah had a conversation with the Lord.

1. Incline your ear to me, O Lord, and hear;

2. Open Your eyes, O Lord, and see; and hear all of the threats that the enemy has used to taunt and to haunt me and to defy even you, the living God.

   The circumstance:

   It is true, O Lord, that the enemy has killed many off with depression, addiction, hopelessness, bitterness, and even suicide. He has caused many to lose confidence in themselves and lose faith in You. As a result, many have not survived what is in this Inventory.

3. Now O Lord, save me from the enemy and all of his threats.

4. Save me so that I will know and fully realize that I am free because You alone, Lord, are God.

PART III: LET IT GO

That was brave. Now we are going to LET IT GO. What about moments when your are driving, or at work, and these negative thoughts pop into your head? How do I let it go? Let's do this:

- For everything on your inventory list that is weighing you down, I want you to create your own, positive affirmation. For instance, if you wrote down, "I'm afraid that I'm always going to be alone," I want you to write: "I am a thoughtful, loving person who is capable and worthy of love. I am too blessed to let negative thoughts defeat me."

- Write down a moment where God answered a prayer. For instance, I want you to write: "God, thank you for restoring my financial profile after I ruined my credit with irresponsible spending," or whatever is relevant for you.

- Write down what you envision God's answer will look like once it is manifested in your life. For instance, I want you to write: "God, I thank you for giving me peace and courage to forgive _____ for hurting me."

- Every time a negative thought pops into your head, declare one of your affirmations and *visualize* it. Do this every single time and before long, you will start to believe and once you believe it in your heart and mind, you will start to see true change in your life.

This exercise is a powerful resolve to drop our fists and raise our hands. This principle is a life-changing attitude. It is perfected with practice. It becomes permanent with consistency.

Dropping Our Fists...

Dropping our fists is the action of humbling ourselves. This is not a science or an art; it is just an action. The only prerequisite for taking this action is our will. We can come to a "done place" with *any* circumstance or situation. Some people successfully complete 12-Step Programs while others may benefit more from counseling or coaching programs that help them to reach their willingness to drop their fists. People with high blood pressure, high cholesterol or diabetes can improve their condition by changing life habits, exercising and eating healthy. Making the decision to change is the first step towards dropping our fists. Or, we can hit what some vernaculars refer to as "bottom" because we become tired of our condition. Notice that all of these *actions* are accomplished by *our* will and not necessarily because of divine enlightenment or spiritual change.

In the Bible, Saul reached his "done place" on the road to Damascus. The Prodigal Son hit bottom after he squandered his inheritance and his self-worth to the extent that he was living among pigs. Peter experienced his "done place" when he denied Jesus shortly after the Last Supper. Judas

Iscariot experienced bottom when he sold Jesus off for 30 pieces of silver. Have you ever reached your "done place" or hit your bottom?

REFLECTIONS

What is the difference between the Bible characters of Saul, the Prodigal Son, Peter, Judas Iscariot and you?   In the stories of Saul, the Prodigal Son and Peter, their done place or bottom experience caused them to deal with the truth of their hearts and come to themselves. As a result, they either established or restored their relationship with God and others. We "come to ourselves" when we wake up, come to a cross road, see the plight of our condition and realize that we have to change. Judas Iscariot never came to himself to realize how to be restored or how to establish a relationship with the Lord. Instead, he found no hope and committed suicide.

Now of course, there are the deep and mystical folk who say that the dichotomy between these examples was due to prophecy and divine order. I challenge that notion because everyone is given the freedom to choose. The element of choice was not taken away from those characters just as it is not taken away from us. God's sovereignty depicted the end from the beginning of how Jesus' death and resurrection would occur, (including the detailed dynamics), but that did not take away personal choice.

The condition of a person's heart makes the difference. Everyone sitting at the table with Jesus began to search themselves and question the motive of their heart when He announced that the person who was going to betray him was sitting with him at the table. Several disciples asked, "Is it me?" I can imagine the fear that swept over the room because all of the disciples understood their shared commonality, the freedom of *choice*. The condition of Judas' heart made him easy prey for the enemy to use him against Jesus.

How does our heart influence what we believe and what we surrender to? Let's review God's plan of salvation to understand the role our heart plays in the most crucial decision of our life.

That if thou shalt confess with thy mouth the Lord Jesus, and shalt believe in thine heart that God hath raised Him from the dead, thou shalt be saved. For with the heart man believes unto righteousness; and with the mouth confession is made unto salvation.

—Romans 10:9-10

The ability to change is within a person's heart. Dropping our fists is also a condition of the heart.

Have you ever asked yourself why a person is so bent on being arrogant, abusive, mean or just indifferent? It is the condition of their heart. On the other hand, have you ever met a forgiving, loving, patient and genuinely kind person who just seems to have a positive attitude about most things? This is the condition of their heart. There are life-changing stories of people who are willing and able to forgive people who committed heinous crimes against them or their families. Where do they get the courage and the empowerment to forgive to the extent that they actually meet the assailant and extend love to them? Their heart.

A heart that chooses to trust God in the middle of adversity is a strong one.

Don't Deflect - Drop

"Drop Your Fists" is challenging us to a higher level of understanding and heart-response. It is challenging us to accept responsibility for our choices. It is reaffirming our accountability to make a change. The enemy wants to keep us blinded by what we see, especially blind to who we see in our mirror. He is always after our spiritual sight to distract us by the who, the why, and the where. If our weapons are not carnal (in the natural realm) then our battle is not carnal. And if the battle is not carnal, it is spiritual.

There are four US Military Branches: Army, Navy, Air Force and Marines. The Army does not teach privates to battle in the air. The Air Force does not train privates to battle in the water. The

Navy and Marines do not train their troops to primarily battle on dry land. Each branch is extensively trained to operate weapons in a specific realm so that they will be masters in using the strategy to defeat the enemy in battle. They are called to fight where the battle is.

God is calling us to fight where the battle is. The battle is in the spirit.

For we wrestle not against flesh and blood, but against principalities, against powers, against the rulers of darkness of this world, against spiritual wickedness in high places.

—Ephesians 6:12 (KJV)

The challenge we have is not to "deflect." It is sometimes easier to make excuses or to just change directions when life becomes uncomfortable or frustrating. Deflecting too soon out of a situation may bring misfortune. Just think about it. What if Jesus had deflected?

You see, God even uses our suffering to birth something new. It is important not to hop in and out of anything too soon even if it causes us to "feel some type of way." God can get the Glory when we suffer awhile, and we always benefit.

In the Bible, God used Saul's jealousy and irrational rage to develop David, his target of unwarranted revenge. He used Nebuchadnezzar, an arrogant king, to fortify three Hebrew boys. He used Darius, a wavering king, to elevate Daniel. God often used Israel's enemies to chastise and discipline them back into righteousness. Just like He did in the Bible days, today, God will use adverse circumstances, conditions, and people to prune our spiritual branch. The level of anointing will determine the height of our opposition. If we bear light afflictions, we will have a featherweight anointing. But if we have endured hellish life battles, we will have a heavyweight anointing. God gets the best out of our worst. He gives the greatest victory through our most painful trials. The secret is knowing that His strength is made perfect in our weakness. For this cause, don't deflect, but "Drop em!"

In our weakness, we may drop our fists and raise our hands. This is most likely what the weak place was purposed for. We will live in and out of these opportunities. Let's not deflect but let's learn to drop. You don't need to church hop, job hop or relationship belly flop to drop your fists. All you need to do is stand still and see the salvation of the Lord work it out in your favor.

Open Net

It is our instinct to avoid harm or pain. We may be willing to turn the other cheek, but it does not mean we won't flinch or lift our fists to dodge or block. It is natural for us to experience anguish. Unfortunately, it has also become normal to adapt to the broken places to the degree that we do not seek healing, long for a way out, or believe that God has more for us beyond the hurt.

Our generation seems to be callousing into a condition where we feel weak for being hurt, scared or angry. As a result, we are taught to self-medicate.

Self-medicating is seeking to relieve our pain through self-pleasures that do not fix or resolve anything, but band aids the pain for the moment and adds more pain once the band aid is removed. Do we need to describe self-medicating band aids? Okay, let's: random acts of sex; excessive alcohol binging; excessive non-prescribed or prescription medication use; other illicit drug use; doing anything that can hurt yourself or others.

In the church, we are sometimes perceived less of a Christian for having feelings of retaliation. We are not being taught the proper rules of engagement; how to deal with our emotions, our setbacks, our set ups and our challenges. As a result, we are being ignored and left with the smorgasbord of the enemy's delicacies to help ourselves. A smorgasbord is a wide range of attractive offerings that offer no real return. For example, Facebook, Twitter, and other social mediums have become a way for people to vent, throw off on others and indirectly deal with their hurt or pain. This is not the proper way to heal or to resolve an issue. This is talking behind raised fists, fighting the air and wasting time. It is also exhausting.

There are more people being misdiagnosed with psychological disorders when they seem emotionally unstable, irrational or overly anxious and depressed. I would challenge that some of these behaviors are actually a condition of a closed heart. Closed for fear of being hurt, ridiculed or judged. I have learned to embrace that it is ok to cry. It is ok to express vulnerability. It is empowering to tell ourselves the truth and to talk to someone else about it. It is empowering to open your heart. It is refreshing and it is liberating. Of course, there are risks associated when sharing *us* with someone else besides the Lord, but I accept that the benefits of freedom far outweighs the fight to get there. I believe Paul explained it best.

I consider that our present sufferings are not worth comparing with the glory that will be revealed in us.

—Romans 8:18

Let's be clear and talk about what *dropping our fists* is not and then let's discover what it *truly* means and how it will bless our lives.

Dropping your fists is not:

- Refusing to acknowledge hurt. As a matter of fact, it is just the opposite. To drop our emotional fists, we have to be willing to acknowledge our hurt.
- Masking emotional pain. Dropping our fists removes the masks so that we can see clearly enough to move in the right direction.
- Mind over matter foolery. This is not a quick remedy or a pack of emotional escape tricks. This is about facing inner truths and making conscious and healthy decisions.
- Magic or Witchcraft. Dropping our fists is not a hocus pocus relief solution.
- A response to a Tarot Card reading. Dropping our fists is not influenced by an outside force, manipulation or calculation. It is a condition of our heart.
- Bleeding out and dumping. Dropping our fists is about acknowledging our own hurts and not just bleeding out and dumping our unresolved issues without an intent to learn how to change our perceptions, our behaviors and perhaps our personalities.
- Entrapping Others. Dropping our fists is not about entrapping others with our "stuff." It is not to hold anyone hostage to what may have contributed to our raised fists. Our fists are raised because we raised them and

not because someone forced us to. It is a strategy for us to free ourselves of weights, baggage, fears, angers, emotional walls, past issues, anxiety, stress and strains that should not be a lasting part of our lives.

MEANINGFUL MOMENTS
PART 1

Stop, Drop and Raise! Sometimes the plight of our circumstance requires immediate resolution and re-direction in order to survive. Sometimes we have to push past fear in the turbulence of life and apply oxygen to our mindset. Regardless of how much pressure we may find ourselves under, we cannot afford to lose our heads. This was my outlook when I resolved to secure the strength of my mind while my heart was torn asunder.

After less than six weeks of marriage, Blind Spot confessed that he was tucking in a young female every night with text messages, phone calls and such. This was the young sister of a family friend he introduced me to while we were courting. This girl was front and center at our wedding. He went on to free himself by letting me know that four months before our wedding, he began sleeping with another woman (and continued the infidelity throughout our entire engagement). To add insult to injury, he also revealed that he had been intimately involved with several women at his job during our courtship and engagement. Not sure how many of these women were included on his guest list to our wedding.

After he was done confessing, he sat back and sighed with relief. Now, I was numb and felt breathless for awhile, but when I came to, the response that came out of me was one that required repentance. I quickly took a trip to the courthouse and made an appointment with spiritual leadership to discuss my intent to annul the marriage due to non-disclosures, deception, and disgust. During our appointment, I was counseled against getting the annulment and pleaded with to allow him to go through therapy. Against everything in me, I agreed.

What happened only six months later without any follow-up, counsel, or accountability was astonishing: spiritual leadership determined that My Blind Spot, who had recently obtained a ministry license, was ready to shepherd a church. The decision was said to be made because "I was there beside him, to support and teach him." There was no caution or accountability to ensure that he was actually in therapy, in a healthy place, or delivered from his proclivities in order to take on the spiritual oversight of others. Even at my request to have at least some level of mentorship or oversight, or better yet, to bring in someone more seasoned, he was appointed. Of course, Blind Spot did not reveal that he was not in therapy or that he was not ready on many levels to shepherd lives because his personal issues were not resolved and his marriage was a mirage. Therefore, once the installation took place, so did the downward spiral of his attitude and the upward climb of the in-home battle. Hot mess! I had heard of the many horror stories of Pastor's wives, and I had even ministered to several distraught women in this position; therefore, I knew of their plight. Now, I found myself like them, in the middle of a bad soap opera, trying to cover and protect the innocent parishioners while in and out of therapy – urgent cares with their Pastor, my Blind Spot. This went on for several years undetected by the congregation because it was embarrassing to me and dangerous for them because they trusted in a system that was collapsing behind the scenes.

After some time, I needed to strengthen my mind to prevent depression, agony, and defeat. I redirected my attention and enrolled in a Master's Program. It was definitely the re-direction that took my mind off the matter at large, almost killed my mind in fact. I had not been in school for 18 years and here I was fully engrossed in a Master of Science Program. I felt good, challenged and free at the same time. It took prayer, more prayer, encouraging friends, tears and sleepless nights before I mastered the time-management skills required for on-line education. I still managed my home life, church life and work life. My passion was my children and my education. The mechanics of my marriage were still intact, including the physical intimacy. Some appetites do not change with pain;

they just feast differently. I became numb to his rejection, emotional abuse, loss of conviction and embarrassing antics.

With the MS Program, I had something new to focus on, something positive to talk about, new people to glean from and new funnels of freedom. I was surviving and thriving at the same time. During this time, I also went through a certified coaching program. I was establishing a new place and more space for God to fill. I was expanding my scope to change careers and direction.

I reached out to his "spiritual superiors" (the term he used for spiritual leadership) for help almost every month for several years, alerting that there was "smoke on aisle five that needed immediate attention." By the time the fire was full blown, the rescue caravan rushed in, but it was clearly too late. I was trying to protect the church from public shame and prevent them from knowing that their leader was not capable of leading them. Blind Spot resigned, unseasoned saints scattered like sheep in the field and leadership did not recover the lost sheep.

I was asked to be a band-aid to this massacre by leadership, but I refused in order to avoid becoming a casualty. The anointing is not to be pimped; meaning that we have to be careful not to allow people to put us in positions or situations that benefit *their* agenda at *our* expense. When this is attempted, our assignment is clearly over!

Private emotional abandonment and public shame were the consequences of allowing someone to drive broadside in my blind spot. But I refused to die there.

After his resignation from the church, My Blind Spot continued to play video games, text women, and appeared to fall into a deep depression. He decided that our marriage and the other life responsibilities he had chosen were "too hard." His resolve was to sell our house, which was leaking and falling apart, and to resign from our marriage. I had to make some decisions. Once I graduated from the Master's Program, I had a moment to exhale and regroup. Through counsel from close friends and prayer, I decided to take the offer to pursue a Ph.D. program that was extended to me by my university.

I will continue this story in my next installments of Meaningful Moments, but in the meanwhile, let's discuss what dropping our fists involves.

Dropping our fists means operating against the norm. It also involves:

- <u>Opening the deepest part of our hearts</u>. Dropping our fists indicates that we are aware and willing to admit we are hurting or in pain.

- <u>Letting down the defense</u>. This means that we are dropping our guard to acknowledge that a person or a situation causes us to feel trapped, unsafe, exposed, and uncomfortable.

- <u>Letting Go of Dead Weight</u>. We have to be willing to go through the eye of the needle. The eye of the needle is actually a Needle Gate believed to be in Jerusalem. For security, the entrance is extremely narrow and low to the ground, requiring the camel to be stripped of any saddles or packs. Hate is a weight. Another person's spouse that we are involved with emotionally or physically is a weight. Bitterness is a weight. Addiction, regardless of what kind, is a weight. Just like the camel, we have to be willing to let go of our saddles or packs.

MEANINGFUL MOMENTS PART 2

My father was diagnosed with Alzheimer's Dementia and I was faced with the decision to become his conservator. Dad was writing blank checks to himself, ordering manifold products from Publishing Clearing House in both of our names, crashing his car, putting his groceries into his closet then calling me, demanding that I bring back his purchased items. My brother had detected our dad's decline, but I had difficult time accepting it. Dad owned property and had other business dealings that were active and declining. Dad would agree to let me assist him and then would call and attack me over the phone about issues we never discussed. He declined swiftly, forgetting to take his medications and eating spoiled food which landed him in the hospital close to death several times. I sought legal counsel and began the process of conservatorship. My father became abusive and aggressive during this process. As a result, we were in court proceedings, visiting therapists for his mental assessments, and bombarded with Veteran Administration (VA) visits almost weekly. Dad fought the idea of conservatorship relentlessly until he had an almost fatal experience. During one of his VA appointments, his doctor encouraged me to let them take over his care by putting him in a VA extended care center 85 miles away to keep him comfortable so that I could go on and live my life in peace. Dad was present and very much coherent. He was forgetful but not deaf and certainly not void of understanding fundamental concepts. I looked at my dad's countenance when the doctor gave me the advice. He dropped his head in shame. My heart was immediately changed toward my daddy. I told the doctor that he was *my* responsibility and that my *peace* was to take care of him. My Dad's heart changed at that moment; he became a humbled, weepy, yet feisty, child-like individual who trusted and depended upon me for his life.

After several failed home-care alternatives, I put dad in a senior home where my daughters, my close friend and I visited with him often. When dad went into renal failure after about two years, it was determined by his physician, my attorney, my daughters and I, to let death take its proper order in his life. This was hard. My Dad helped to raise both of my daughters. He was their Grandpa, but he was also their father-figure, especially for my oldest because her father refused to foster a relationship with her. While he was in hospice, he indicated that he had "taken care of his soul business and was now excited." This was monumental indeed. To God be the glory! The entire arduous process was humbling, breaking and profound for me. I had dropped my fists and let go of so much hurt, past pain, resentment and the negative images. As Daddy's Little Girl, I saw my father as my hero, the one that sheltered me, picked me up and carried me long after I could walk, the one who made me feel pretty when I dressed up, and the one who taught me that I never had to beg or become uncomfortable to be treated like a princess. Somewhere along the way; however, my hero turned into a monster without notice and explanation. For years, I resented him for my mother's broken heart, my brother's drug addiction, and my struggle to find love in a man. But, once I dropped my fists and raised my hands, all I could see was my "Daddy," my Hero! It was amazing!

CHAPTER BREAK

CHAPTER 4
RAISE YOUR HANDS

Dropping our fists is an action we take because we acknowledge and accept our need to be free from whatever has incapacitated our ability to heal. Dropping our fists encourages us and strengthens us to thrive, strive and soar. It is a unique experience—personal, private and on purpose. Raising our hands is also a unique experience; however, it requires much more than just recognition and acceptance of our position. Raising our hands recognizes and accepts *God's* position. This poses the question, not just what, but *where* is the Lord's position in our life?

Dropping our fists may not result from a spiritual experience or encounter and it is not required for this action to take place in our lives. God always plays an integral part in the lives of people whether they acknowledge, recognize, or realize His presence. One may drop their emotionally, spiritually, or otherwise raised fists for many reasons as discussed earlier.

Raising our hands, however, absolutely denotes spiritual enlightenment, a personal spiritual encounter, experience, or epiphany, because it is an act of surrender to the Lord, Jesus Christ. This action requires one to willingly respond by recognizing, realizing, receiving, and *then* raising.

Recognize

Recognizing God is an interesting concept. I believe what makes idolatry easier to conform to is its tangibility. People desire serenity through and by some "thing" and not necessarily with some "one." People seem to find it easier to attach, associate with and devote themselves to something that does not require maintaining a relationship, costs nothing and requires no surrender or a need for change, especially in this world of greed and speed.

Divinity is sought through mediums of ease, non-invasive things and inanimate objects rather than through what may prove to be alive and real, yet distant. It is hard to see God past ourselves. To recognize God, we have to first recognize ourselves, our true selves, with the manifold frailties, flaws, and fragments.

Recognizing ourselves requires identification. Who are we really? Underneath the several surfaces that we wear, who are we? Have we identified *who* we are without trying to add or subtract the abstract? Who are we at the *core*? Have we identified who we are without the roles that we play, the responsibilities we own and the accountabilities we live to fulfill? Have we distinguished our uniqueness beyond our frame? People who have not recognized themselves have a difficult time recognizing the Lord. Not just believing that He exists, but acknowledging that He exists in *every* essence of our lives. It is the process of "knowing," the meaning of life. It sounds complicated, and on some level it is. We are complex, fearfully and wonderfully made in God's image and in His likeness. To figure us out then, is to figure God out and we will never do that, but we can recognize Him. We can know Him, we can identify Him and we can distinguish Him. God is a gentleman; however, His truth is invasive because it challenges our thoughts, our will, and our mindset without apology. This is the demonstration of how God is relational, loving us enough to reveal our inner truths and covering us while we face them.

Our recognition of God happens when we believe in our hearts. Whatever we prioritized in our belief is diminished when we recognize God. Whatever we depended upon as our point of reference for dealing with our life's problems is destroyed when we recognize God. Whatever we thought, perceived or acknowledged as our deity (anything or anyone that is not Jesus Christ, the Lord), is mortified when we recognize God. And to get to raising our hands, we have to go this way, we have to recognize God.

*Be still and know that I am God; I will be exalted
among the nations; I will be exalted in the earth.*

—Psalm 46:10 (NIV)

God draws us into a stillness to recognize who
He is. A stillness of our heart and mind, which frees
us from anxiety. God ushers us into this serene
place so that we are *clear* to identify His deity and
distinguish Him above *all* else.

Realize

After we recognize God, we have to come to a
place of absolute clarity and awareness. We also
need to possess an unequivocal resolve that Jesus
Christ is God's Son and there is no name under
Heaven by which mankind can be "saved" and
reconciled to God. This becomes fact just like the
DNA of who we are. This becomes our belief that
cannot be compromised, manipulated or
diminished. We have to come to this place of
conviction that the Lord is one God and Father of
all, who is over all and through all and in all
(Ephesians 4:6, (NIV).

Realizing God is realizing our very existence is
of God. This realization begins the humbling
process before we resolve to raise our hands. This
is when we graduate beyond recognizing God and
truly adopt that He *is* God and it is *He* that has
made us and not we, not Darwin, not Science, not
Astrology and not any other natural or unnatural

thing, has made us. We are His people and symbolized as the sheep in His pasture, invited to enter into His very presence with adoration and unto His intimate space with our praise.

We realize God as we open our hearts and our minds to His enlightenment, illumination, and understanding. We do this by openly acknowledging Him internally, within our heart of hearts by faith. We humbly provoke Him to prove Himself by inviting Him *in* to save *our*selve*s*. This happens because we realize Him. When we realize Him, we open our mouths and confess Him. We confess that Jesus is Lord. We then believe in our hearts by faith that He was crucified for the sins of the world, and more specifically, for our personal sins and that God raised Him from the dead.

Based upon this realization resulting in this confession, we are "saved." Saved from what? The penalty of sin, the power of sin and the essence of sin. This does not prevent us from sinning or falling into sin, but it provides mercy and grace for us not to stay there.

Receive

A consistent "giver" typically has a difficult time receiving. Those of us who have been rejected, hurt, defamed, abased or abandoned on any level sometimes do not know *how* to receive. And, some people who have calloused their hearts with pride because they have been fighting to prove their worth or to be accepted, definitely struggle with receiving.

Some feel undeserving of receiving because they feel that it will somehow make them powerless. All of these impediments to receiving are fallacies that prevent us from receiving the ONLY true gift of God, salvation through his Son, Jesus Christ. It is FREE, it is by His grace, leaving NO one to boast or take any glory or credit for it. The only action required is to receive it. How? By opening your heart and your mouth.

For with the heart man believeth unto righteousness; and with the mouth confession is made unto salvation.

—*Romans 10:10*

Receiving from a sincere heart requires a level of humility. It is interesting that receiving would require humility because after all, we are not pouring out or giving of ourselves at that moment. Receiving requires humility because we have to position our hearts to take in and to be poured into. What is received may not be material possessions; it may be forgiveness or an apology from someone or an act of kindness that we clearly do not deserve.

How do we position our hearts to receive? By opening up. We must open our hearts and sometimes our minds in order to receive from someone else. This may sound like commonplace stuff, but it is not always that easy. When I look back over the things I have done in my life, I sometimes have a difficult time receiving God's choice blessings because I feel undeserving of them. I came to an impasse while studying the concept of "double portion" in the Bible. I cannot imagine deserving a double portion of blessings. I am not worthy of it! When I started receiving several words of encouragement that confirmed this over my life, I did not believe it. Not because I doubted God, but because I knew better about myself. I am coming to realize that receiving is not about deserving but more about gifting; God blesses us based upon His grace and His will and not our right or reason. It is His choice. Our job is to receive it with humility, rejoice in it and be a good and faithful steward over it.

We will never out give God or match His giving to us or be able to comprehend *why* He gives to us. The only thing we can give in return is our all. We can lay down our all by raising our hands.

COMMERCIAL BREAK

Have you considered all? I have taught and preached about this concept several times from different vantage points. The question can have more than one meaning depending on the context and the intent.

First, let's discover "all" as a concept of total surrender. All, in this context, denotes everything, nothing spared, kept back, held up or reserved. It means all in, all or nothing, complete, and entire. This is a question to ponder before getting married, having children, or most importantly, choosing a relationship with Jesus Christ. It is a choice, an act of faith and a lifelong process of giving up ourselves. This "all" is weathered, tethered and worn, but empowering. It is mature, sacrificial, open, honest and secure. This *all* is often at the end of everything else tried, the final frontier, the bottom of our bottom and the end of our end.

Now, let's discover *all* from the perspective of cost. *All* in this context is associated with value, capacity, and consequence. *All* challenges us to make a decision with an understanding of what is at stake, what is required, and what is expected.

When I felt as though I had nothing left to give emotionally or mentally, God gave me the capacity to give my *all* from a *poor in spirit place*. Being *poor in spirit* is feeling empty and like you have nothing to look forward to. It is, perhaps, meant to be a humbling place, but not meant to be humiliating. Yet, at times, it feels humiliating, especially if this place is witnessed by others. Giving our all is not about what we have, but it is more about being willing to surrender all that we have; ourselves. In spite of feeling empty, I was still able to muster up enough strength to give attention to my children when I felt like a failure before them. If all I had to give was attention because my financial situation was limited, God knew now to satisfy them with my *all*. It was in *this* place that I learned how God makes up for our shortage when we surrender.

God knows best how to encourage us and give us strength. When I felt that my all was not enough, but God made it bigger to the person receiving from me: my kids would thank me for cooking for them, my co-workers would compliment my efforts and others would testify of a time when I said something to encourage them. My *all* seemed limited because I felt poor; defeated, exhausted, and sometimes, numb. Just when I needed it, God would bless me with someone to lift my spirit with an unexpected financial gift, encouragement, or opportunity.

When we surrender our all, God gives us what we need. I am learning the season of "all" is the place where we have to push past our hurt, our feelings of inadequacy, and our proclivity to give up.

Have you considered all? I encourage you to trust God if you are in a poor in spirit place and watch Him work things out for your good.

Raise Your Hands

Once we have dropped our fists, we need an anchor to remain established, strengthened and settled. That anchor can be the act of raising our hands. Notice that I did not say to just dance, shout, or take a duck-walk lap around the church. Now, this does not mean that we should not do any of those powerful expressions of praise, but let's not get stuck there. Let's not discount a full response that includes permanent change, new direction, new resolve and a new opportunity.

A committed relationship is not meant to be consummated in public. The declaration may be public, but the consummation is private. We may give God glory openly through testimonials or, if we are of the charismatic persuasion, we may lift Him straight up in a dance, but when we are by ourselves and the music is gone, and the people are not present, we need to spiritually consummate our relationship with the Lord. When we are alone, purposely in a quiet place and still, it is the best time to have "face-time" with God.

Face-time with God can happen while sitting up, standing still, or kneeling. My preference is lying out on the floor prostrate. It is a humble stance, a change in position that denotes something different has happened in our life, and further, that something is *about* to transpire. There should be a different internal and external posture when engaging God on an intimate level. We should have an humble approach to become pliable and adaptable. Once we are submerged into this face-time place, we are in His intimate space.

Now, raise up! Raise your hearts in adoration, in awe and in worship. Tell the Lord what He has meant to you, even if it is not all clear, realized or understood. Tell Him what He has meant to you before you dropped your fists. Tell Him how this principle affected your relationship with Him. Tell Him what it did for you. Tell Him what he has meant to you over the years and how much His presence made a difference in your life. Come in close and tell Him the truth of what is in your heart.

Now tell Him what He currently means to you. Express what you believe to be the advantages of being His child, even if they are not all recognized yet, express your anticipation of them. Tell Him what you look forward to with Him, because of Him and now that He is within you. Tell Him what He means to you *right now, today*. Tell Him what fears you have overcome because of Him. Tell Him what hurts, pains and doubts you have released because of Him.

This is raised hands.

We raise our hands as a sign that our hearts are lifted. This does not by any means exclude the paralyzed or those without the ability to physically raise a portion of their body. God embraces raised hearts based upon a raised awareness. This is an intimate process. This is the process of looking up. King David understood this intimate gesture.

I will lift up mine eyes unto the hills from whence cometh my help. My help cometh from the Lord, which made heaven and earth.

—Psalm 121:1-2

The importance of raising our hands to God is surrender. When our hands are raised, it is difficult to have a hung down head. Raising our hands causes our head to lift also. Looking up will cause us to raise up.

The act of raising our hands requires determination, especially when we become weary, worn and just plain tired with life's challenges, situations, and circumstances. This is not a one-time action, just like dropping our fists is not a one-time action.

Raising our hands is a paradigm shift to the way we respond to the battle called life. When we raise our hands to the Lord, it is just like a child raising their hands to their parent. Children desire to be picked up when they want to see something from a safe and higher level, when they are afraid or when they are unsure. This childlike gesture is embraced by our Heavenly Father. He desires to be our source for everything, for all things and forever.

Raised hands is an indication that we have surrendered our trust to God because we realize that He is worthy of our absolute faith.

When Jesus was in the Garden of Gethsemane approaching God before His imminent crucifixion, He had face-time. During His face-time, He dropped His fists and surrendered His will to God. During His face-time, He was able to resist His natural tendency to raise His fists. Like Jesus, no one wants to suffer hurt, pain or anguish; and, certainly not publicly. When we find ourselves in hard life situations we must follow this example.

Now, we all know the victory Jesus experienced by dropping His fists and raising His hands because we live it out every day. Jesus understood His purpose but that did not prevent Him from raising His hands. He knew that His closest companions, the disciples, would forsake Him in some form or another, but He raised his hands. His natural parents could not prevent or stop what was about to happen to Him. Not only could they not stop the madness, they also had to sit back and watch while the many He healed, delivered, fed, saved and restored, would cry out against Him. Nevertheless, He raised His hands. He could not even ask for more time. He was born on death row. He came to die, for us: the unfaithful, the fallible, the unthankful, the unholy, the perverted, the selfish, the heartless, the aloof, the unappreciative, the unregenerate, the trucebreakers, the hypocrites, and the ignorant. He dropped His fists and raised His hands. He struggled. He cried. He anguished. He lamented. He even asked God to explore another alternative. But, during the process, His conclusion was to raise His hands, "Nevertheless, not my will, but thine will be done."

We are not cut from the same cloth as Jesus, so the scenarios we face may not emulate His experiences, but the expectation is the same: Drop Your Fists and Raise Your Hands.

REFLECTIONS

Raising your hands in surrender to the Lord will free your will, your heart and your mind to a new beginning, but it may also release people from your life who are not connected to your purpose. There are people who cannot go with you into your purpose although they may have promised to, perhaps acted like they intended to or may have truly thought they could. Any relationship has to be built upon more than the *moment*.

Now, the foundation for romantic relationships should be developed with a vision for the *end of life* and not just for the honeymoon phase of life. I have experienced relationships that seemed like a great connection initially. Hey, three men actually believed that they loved me enough to marry me. I have been known as "a good thing." The woman who seems to have it all together with a good job, easy on the eyes, strong, dependable, and a great supporter—a really *good idea*.

I have learned that I am more than a "good idea." I am more than a moment, a side-piece, my accomplishments, my looks, a casual quest or conquest meant to be won or tamed. That devil is a lie! And now that *I* know that, those who attempt to approach me will discover it too. You see, people perceive you and treat you based upon the way you allow them to because of self-personifications. If we are only partially together, internally weak, fronting self-esteem and too busy to self-care, we may give off a scent of vulnerability that attracts vultures. The nature of the vulture is to lie in wait on their prospective prey, to study their non-alert habits, pick up on their fears, and to catch them off their guard in order to lure them away for the kill. Raising our hands to the Lord puts us in a new life-set, not just a new mindset, and therefore changes our *scent*. We no longer have the scent of one who is thirsty for attention, hungry for a compliment, or desperate for companionship. We are hidden behind God's protective seal and can only be *discovered* as God opens divine doors. The challenge then becomes waiting for an opportunity for a healthy relationship and having the patience to wait until we are discovered.

A divine release happens when we understand that people who are mutually committed to you and therefore attached to you on purpose and for a purpose, cannot leave you. This concept applies to *all* relationships in our lives. *If* anyone *can* leave you—let them go. Anyone that walks away from you because the connection becomes a challenge, too hard, inconvenient or uncomfortable for *them*—let them walk. A divine release is to raise our hands to our Heavenly Father and ask Him to pick us up and out of harm's way. This may involve a divine release from people, all people (dropping the mic).

The Power of Release

How does the power of release tie into raising our hands in surrender to the Lord? Often times, one-sided ties that bind us to people prevent us from raising our hands because it deters our focus. One-sided relationship ties are the connections that we may have to people who have already disconnected from us, whether it be emotional, mental, physical or spiritual. People often stay bound to someone who has released *them* long ago because it is uncomfortably comfortable. The connection is familiar and sometimes easy, even if it no longer benefits or fits into our life, our aspirations or our purpose. This happens in all types of relationships. To let go of someone we deem close to us seems difficult if we have formed a *habit* of connection. A habit of connection refers to the mechanics of being present while our heart or the other person's heart is not fully invested.

When do we release them and how does it look? Well, this can be complicated. Having the "gift of goodbye" is empowering when we have the strength, fortitude, and wisdom to walk away from abusive relationships or connections. The gift of goodbye is the ability to let people and things go that bring us down without looking back or picking it back up again. Not only does the person or situation not add value to our lives, they are a liability to our future. Goodbye is a power-statement. Once we begin to release ourselves from liabilities, we will fill our lives with meaningful investments.

We have to raise our hands to the Lord and seek Him for direction. Yes, raising our hands involves much more than just spiritual enlightenments; it will involve our entire *self* to engage in the process of *alignment*. We release to God, and He blesses us. We draw nigh to God, and He draws nigh to us. We seek God, and He covers us. We reach out to Him, and He reaches *inside* of us. Although the *value* of what we give versus what we receive is clearly not equal, the process is still required. As we move into a closer relationship with the Lord, we will change, and this is the first indication of alignment.

God will begin to change our perspective to align it with His. This alignment process may not be definable or even explainable, but it becomes measurable over time. God will begin to change our surroundings and we may find ourselves among people or in places that we did not solicit, anticipate or consider. This is alignment. God will change atmospheres when we enter into them by changing the conversation, redirecting a decision or providing a platform for you to share. This is alignment. God will heal your frame of mind toward a particular situation without you even putting forth any anxiety to force or make the feelings change. This is alignment. God may ultimately uproot you and plant you into a new opportunity or situation that you did not push, apply for or position yourself for. This is alignment. And then, of course, there is the exchange where God will give you a miracle portion of strength to get out of something that is clearly not safe. Again, this is divine alignment. These are all examples of the power that comes with divine release. Power is having the authority to change the rules. Earlier we discussed the rules of engagement. There may come a time in your life when God will change the rules or give you the strength to change the rules in your life. If addiction had a hold on you, God will give you the power to change that rule in your life and you will act in the power of release. If a long lasting painful memory collides with your process of raising your hands, the rules will change and you will find the power of release from it. There really is no answer for how the alignment takes place or even when it takes place sometimes. We will walk into it or walk away from it. Sometimes subtly and at other times, aggressively. Powerful nevertheless.

Shaking Off a Lot

With good intentions, have we taken in or otherwise connected to someone or something that we need to *shake off*? Most of the time, we need to shake them off because there is not enough room for both our purpose and their presence and all that their presence encompasses.

We sometimes feel compelled to save, to take on or to *pack* someone or something into our divine move that God did not intend for us to include. Father Abraham learned this lesson when he, with good intentions, took Lot with him when God spoke his purpose into motion. He packed him into the equation. We have to be careful about what we put into the suitcase of our life. If we have too much unnecessary weight, God will stop us at the divine weight-station and cause us to open our baggage and determine what is valuable and what is not important. That which is not important will have to find its own way.

So Abram departed, as the Lord had spoken unto him; and Lot went with him: and Abram. And Abram took Sarai his wife, and Lot his brother's son, and all their substance that they had gathered, and they went forth to go into the land of Canaan.

—*Genesis 12:4-5.*

Sometimes we take on extra baggage that we find ourselves having to shake off. Lot became too much. God spoke to Abram about uprooting his life to move towards his destiny. This was not a missionary journey; it was a singular move. Abram packed up his family and took his nephew Lot with him because he felt obligated to look after his brother's son. Despite his spiritual heritage, Lot seemed to live on the edge and made decisions that caused some to question his character. He was a disrespected leader in Sodom, a city full of perversion. At some point, Lot would even offer up his daughters for prostitution, but God still stepped in to protect Lot and his family. With all of this chaos, Lot's baggage became a weight for Abraham; and at God's divine weight-station, Abraham and Lot separated. Sometimes we obligate ourselves when and where we shouldn't because of *family* or obligation to someone close to our lives. Some people seem to have a "rescue syndrome" that *compels* them to take on the burdens of others without them even asking. This is the *Family of Lots*. *Lots* are conveniently present, positioned at the bottom of your funnel, and typically non-contributors. These are the people in our family or close circle of friends who always show up for the potluck with a knife and fork, but without a dish or contribution. These are the people we tend to consider and make special provisions for while they sit and fold their hands waiting to be served or rescued. Some of these behaviors are generational and will likely continue forever until someone raises their hands to God and God gives them the power of release.

We have to release ourselves from the Bail Bond habit. Some people seem to take on the lives of others, always bailing them out, to the degree that we stifle them from establishing a relationship with God for themselves. Why do they need to develop their faith in Jesus when we are always there to bail them out? We hinder the work of God in their lives, but more so, we fail to see their heart, their intentions and their weight on our lives. We have to shake off the Lots in our life. Just like Abraham shook off his nephew and had him move away, we have to do the same with those who connect to us to avoid making a way for themselves.

If we are not deliberate with our spiritual stewardship, we can load ourselves down with things that can become a TARE among the wheat in our purpose. Taking on more than what God placed upon us can invite in a Tare, and over time that tare will begin to tear things up. We have to shake off the Lots in our life.

If we do not shake off the Lots, we will become their personal automatic teller machine, their dial-an-out where we are only a phone call away to bail them out of whatever mess they got themselves into. There are people who have created an occupation by taking away from others: time, treasure, talent, and tissue. These are *Tares*. When we raise our hand to God, He will cause us to see the wheat from the tares and begin to pull up the weeds. This sometimes requires a plan, a strategy, or an exodus. The power of release is the process of formulating an exodus to divinely release you from those who take from you. At some point, we need people in our lives that actually contribute, pour into, and provide girth. We need to begin surrounding ourselves with people who can *inspire* us: people who are smart, innovative, accomplished, progressive and prosperous. We have to engage with people who challenge us to improve our standard of living.

MEANINGFUL MOMENTS

As I sat on the bed with my laptop, responding to discussions in the Ph.D. course room, I would find myself engaged in fiery exchanges with my Blind Spot. Most of these exchanges were due to a discovery of his indiscretions. I grew tired of waiting for the other shoe to drop with yet another episode of his unfaithfulness. He would often ask me why I was still there and would often times tell me to do whatever I needed to do because he no longer cared. I would sit there, tears streaming down my face, because I would look around and internally say to God that I did not have the strength to do what it would take to leave. I did not feel that I had the capacity to walk away or to pick up the pieces of my life now that he had walked away emotionally and otherwise. There was a lot of time and "things" that we had invested over the span of a decade. To just up and walk away right in the middle of "life" seemed more than a mountain to speak to; it was overwhelming. And every time the conversation came up, I gave him a reason why I was there: *I still care. I did not come into this with a plan B. I am responsible for us and trying to make this work. Because I love you.* One day, however, as I sat there in that same place about to exchange in battle, my Blind Spot said that he had given me every Biblical reason and release to leave, so why was I yet still there. He was expressing that he had an affair or was currently having one and that was my divine release. When I went to answer him *this* time, God told me not to say anything.

And there I sat, with my mouth open and nothing coming out for a moment. God spoke to me and said that I did not *really* hear what was being said and where it was truly coming from. It was not merely frustration or anger, but a true expression of his heart. I heard God clear and the pain was so relentless that I felt like I could not breathe. On this particular evening, God said it was time for me to go; and in that moment, a strength came over me that I cannot articulate. When I went to work the following morning, I sat down with a notepad and began to write out a plan as if I were taking dictation. I itemized every shared investment, every shared expense, every financial obligation and set deadlines for when these items were to be dissolved, resolved, or revoked.

Blind Spot determined to short-sale our home and walk away from everything, but he was torn between taking his wedding ring on and off. I helped his quandary. I let him know that I had the key to my new place.

For a moment, he was making plans on how *we* would orchestrate our move, but I provided clarification. This was not going to be a traveling circus, praise God. He wanted out, had told me to take everything and just get out at one point, and of course, he was actively texting someone new or someone old, who knows, and I really did not care at this point.

When he realized that he was not moving with me, he told me to choose between the bedroom and living room set. At first I said, "Both! Naked you came into this marriage and naked you shall leave," but I ended up only taking the living room set and other stuff that were inconsequential.

My heart was hurting as I looked at all the investments and memories around our home. I began the transition process. I had to explain my plans to my youngest daughter while not telling my oldest (to keep her from worrying about me while trying to study in college).

That same week, I received a phone call from a company that offered me a position on the side of town where I grew up. To boot, the location was also where my youngest daughter was attending school. I began looking for places to rent on that side of town to accommodate me and the girls. I was blessed with a spacious condominium within walking distance from my new job and my daughter's school.

It happened so quickly that I was surprised by the turn around. I went to the bank and obtained a loan against the equity on one of my vehicles and was able to completely furnish my new place and purchase all new linen, kitchen supplies, and furniture as needed.

I moved right from under Blind Spot without him realizing it because he was preoccupied with ignoring *me* and I did not need any of the everyday items that he would notice missing (like the new leather couch). I planned my exodus for several weeks. I loaded my friend's garage with new furnishings and scheduled deliveries in preparation of move-in day. I was hoping that my Blind Spot would wake up to the love I had for him, but he was gone in many aspects. So, on the morning of my exodus, I attempted a congenial conversation to figure out a way to tell him I was leaving, but he was an emotional wall. God spoke to me and said not to say a word. As he left for work that morning, he brushed passed me aggressively and said, "I'm out!"

I thought, "So am I!"

As soon as he drove away, the exodus began. I dropped my youngest daughter off at our new home so that she could walk to school; then I picked up the moving truck. I was providing ministry at a local rehabilitation center so I was allowed to take residents in and out. I signed up two gentlemen for the day, and together we moved all of the heavy furniture that I could not load and unload myself. I made sure to wash all of his clothes since I was taking the washer and dryer. My friend had to stop me from folding his clothes (I had to leave, but I did not have to leave angry). I was leaving physically, but my heart was still connected because I had the unfinished business of being very much in love with a man who did not want me in his life. People fall in and out of love, but I signed up for a life-sentence. I knew I had to go and I did not want to make it any more painful so I felt compelled to leave "nice." I was hurt, but not angry. I was broken but did not want to become bitter. By the time Blind Spot returned home that day, I was completely moved out. The power of release.

When my daughter came home from school, she came home to a new life with just "us." For the first few weeks, we slept together, a bit uncomfortable in the adjustment. Blind Spot did not call or reach out, and I did not hear from him for several weeks until we had to finalize paperwork toward the short-sale. We were cordial, friendly even. When my oldest came home for Christmas, she walked in our new place, looked around, then said, "Mommy, this is so peaceful!" All three of us held each other and cried. Many close friends and family would visit, and they would all say how much peace was in my home. Sometimes people learn to adapt and adjust to chaos until it feels normal. I guess that had been the case for me.

The Healing After Deliverance

When Israel got out of bondage from Egypt, they were miraculously delivered from Pharaoh. Receiving the healing they needed as a result of that bondage, however, was a different, arduous process. Israel would spend *many* years in emotional bondage after their deliverance. At some point between their deliverance and the promised land, Israel would actually long for the provisions they had while in bondage under Pharaoh's abuse. Of course, this angered God, disappointed the prophets of God and prolonged the many blessings planned for Israel.

Raising our hands will put us in place to not only experience deliverance from or out of something, but it will also begin the healing process from the impact of something that almost took us out. After deliverance comes healing; meaning that the two processes are different. Deliverance is our freedom from something and healing is our freedom to never go back there. If we only come out of negative situations but are never healed from the *impact*, we can be subtly drawn back in. The principle of drop your fists and raise your hands will have to become our profile and practiced response to the battle for us to experience the healing that brings new life. New life in this context means new perspective, new perception, and a new essence. We will have to walk away from the *rule* of victimization and establish the new rule of *responsible empowerment*.

New Perspective

A new perspective can result from taking steps to heal and by being receptive to new opportunities. This is exhilarating because it can be a chance to put things into a new focus and make new plans. A new perspective takes some time to acclimate into, of course, because it is uncharted territory, but we will establish new points of reference. We will be drawn to people who have survived where we are coming out of and who also have the capacity to propel us into developing new appetites. For example, we will seek positive tools to reinforce our new outlook: books, conferences, and such. What satisfied us in the past will no longer be fulfilling, and our emotional palate will have a hunger for edifying and fortifying connections.

There will be naysayers, judgmental folks, gossipers, etc., who do not know what we have survived, struggled in and overcome. They may not even care, and frankly, it will not matter. I had to learn how to avoid explaining myself, apologizing to irrelevant bystanders and to keep living out my new perspective. I had to learn to not allow another person's issue to become my project. I exposed myself to healthy ministry, read inspirational books and engaged in good Christian counseling. After putting this oxygen on my *own* life, I took my girls in for counseling to help them through their issues. Both of my daughters remained emotionally healthy and strong. They agreed to talk to counselors; however, they would let me know that they were okay and did not need to continue. As my girls got older, I would periodically open the opportunity for them to talk to a counselor around the same time they received their physicals. I told them that it was important to be holistically healthy and that I wanted them to take care of their emotions and mindset as well as their body. Through the years, I practiced the same concept. As I matriculated through various rites of passage (death of my parents, pre–menopause.), I would have a session with my counselor.

I had to take time out from connecting to any one ministry for a season. People get so used to you and the added value that you bring, and sometimes they fail to see your heart and your needs. I attended several churches just to sit because I needed to worship and to cry. I was in mourning for a great while after my Blind Spot resigned from pastoring and from our marriage. After I refused the request to take over the leadership of the church within a new system of administration by spiritual leadership, I did not want to be a hindrance to whoever would assume the pastoral role and I needed to convalesce for a season in order to regroup. I needed to go through the grieving process. Several churches would demand that I sit in front, have words of expression or even invite me to provide exhortation while I was openly hyperventilating in tears. Really? It was a nightmare, embarrassing and painful.

Developing a new perspective will reveal who we can trust with our hearts and who we have to hide from. For me, it took separation and reflection. We may not be able to actually *see* ourselves until we separate from people, places and things. I had to separate myself from both negative and seemingly positive influences. Negative people with pessimistic attitudes cannot speak into our lives because they do not have faith, self-satisfaction, or discernment, much less wisdom. For example, I experienced people ridiculing me with a smile, trying to embarrass me or put me on the spot in public, or gossiping about me (instead of talking *to* me) to close associates in order to send me a message. People tend to judge, mock, and speak negatively against what they do not have a clue about. I realized that I needed to stop this madness by disassociating myself from this population, regardless of how close they acted or appeared to be. *Seemingly* positive people will encourage you by giving you an excuse to live beyond your convictions. Anybody who gives you advice that it is ok to partake in behavior that conflicts with the Word of God and your convictions is not good for your life. While I was going through a difficult time in my marriage, people, churched and unchurched, would say things like, "Girl, I would have been in John

Wayne's arms by now…," meaning that they would have cheated with another man while going through a difficult place in their marriage. I had a spiritual leader ask me what I was going to do for *sex* when Blind Spot left me and resigned from pastoring the church. My response to that ridiculous question was simple: "Not you!"

We have to take the time to reflect to avoid repeating bad decisions. I had to think about when and how I allowed myself to get into a position to raise my fists. What was going on in my life, who was I listening to, why was I vulnerable and how did I become such easy prey for the enemy? Reflection allows us to learn something about ourselves to stop us from blaming others, making excuses, or developing a cycle of bad choices. I learned not to make major decisions while going through an emotionally draining situation, not to listen to anyone or anything that provides an easy way out with long-term negative consequences, and not to put myself in situations that will cause me to compromise my convictions. We tend to act unlearned when we want to compromise by telling ourselves *"a little bit won't hurt,"* "God *knows my heart,"* or *"just this one time and then I will stop."* Mercy! We have to separate and reflect in order to develop a new perspective.

New Personification

A new personification is an entire personal renovation, much like overhauling an old condemned building. My life took on several renovations over the years. When I got away from My Escape, I learned that it was ok to embrace the sexy in me. Hold on, this simply means that it was ok to stop dressing the way that I felt. I felt exhausted, overwhelmed, unloved, and certainly unattractive; my style reflected this haggard personification. A woman with much flare, my pastor's wife at that time, encouraged me to embrace my body and all of its curves by tapering my skirts and dresses. I had to learn how to accentuate my body type. I did not have rolls or trolls on my body, so she encouraged me to stop wearing extra undergarments that make be look bulky while I still could and allow the slip in the skirt to be enough. She allowed me and some of the other women going through a hard place in life, but with good jobs, praise God, to purchase some of her wardrobe and shoes, which were elaborate. Over time, I looked better and eventually, began to feel better. I started wearing concealer to take away the bags under my eyes and began investing in my hair by trying different styles (I even added some tracks and color, thank God). New personification!

Embarking upon a new personification will push us into finding a new groove, like a person without rhythm learning to two-step to more than one genre of music. I learned the balance of good nutrition and exercise and even, began teaching Dance Aerobics at a local gym. With this added income, I began personal training with a bodybuilder to tone and further accentuate my frame; both physically and mentally. I redeveloped muscles that I had not used since I stopped competitive baton-twirling and jazz dancing years prior. I lost 30 pounds and looked (and felt) better than I had in a long time.

We will develop a new essence, new passion and a new set of goals; all as a result of dropping our fists and raising our hands. I actually looked different, methodically losing over 30 pounds and feeling great. Even though I continued to hit rough places in life, my new passion for exercise and health did not allow me to stay in a *funk* for too long.

We will begin to look different, and people will notice. New personification may require some demolition work, just like overhauling a building; walls need to come down, floors need to be replaced, and the frame may need some patch work. Sometimes we make too many concessions in the name of *love* or in an effort to change *who* we are in order to keep a person from being who they *truly* are. If a person is perverted with unnatural proclivities, do not compromise who you are because of someone's unreasonable desires or expectations of who *they* want you to be. In raw terms, do not become a hand puppet in somebody else's freak show. We tend to think that if we are more like the fantasy someone has built up in their twisted mindset, we will keep their attention, earn their love or obtain their affection. When people start off liking you the way you are and then over time try to *change* who you are, it is time to go. For instance, Blind Spot would tell me that my hair was *only* attractive if I wore it one way; pulled back off my face in a ponytail or bun. Ummm? I am still young, not in the military, and not always behind the pulpit, so that became boring and raggedy on me, not to mention it took away from my creativity and style. Over time, my sides thinned out and my hairline started behind my temples, so, pulling my hair back looked like I was recovering from an illness. Not cute. This hairstyle, the only one that was attractive, was no longer an option. When I wore different styles, I would get ignored or told that I knew how he liked my hair. That devil is a lie! When people start down a path of trying to change your essence, it is an attempt to control you, which is a form of emotional abuse. Many people simply do not realize this. When this pattern begins, it is time to go.

It took me some time to find out who this *new* woman was without the responsibility of a church, managing the lives of other people, and, life without a husband. I had wardrobe drama, attitude adjustments, and released people that were toxic. My new personification allowed me to meet new and improved people to surround myself with as I established many new positive connections. I was single, and in good physical shape, so I began to dress it up. I did not have the need to wear some of my suits and such, so I gave them away and began buying dresses, ones that fit my frame. I worked out and maintained a healthy image, so it was time to look how I felt. I was healing from the way Spiritual Leadership treated me when Blind Spot left and I refused to take on a position or place that was not healthy for me. I no longer fit into certain clicks and such, so I had to turn down and turn away several ministry invitations for a season. Most times, these invitations were fishing expeditions into my private life, so God led me away from it and gave me new opportunities on different platforms. I have been called to provide training at corporate conferences out of state, confer degrees in services, and speak at other motivational events. Although initially out of my comfort zone, these experiences have been broadening for me, and have also afforded me new opportunities, new connections and new visibility.

Raising our hands changes our personification because it allows God to influence what we tell ourselves. I had to speak affirmations to myself sometimes just to face the days ahead. Once I completed my Ph.D., I had to face the impact of this accomplishment in my work environment; people feeling threatened and intimidated— referring to me as Dr. Wilson in a mocking tone or giving me a confession as to why they did not accomplish *their* educational and other personal goals. I had to recognize that they were jealous, intimidated, and no matter how much I remained the same person I was *before* the degree, their issues would have to be worked out by them. I determined to live with raised hands while they decided to live with raised fists.

Redeveloping our personification is like reincarnating. It is a different type of revival that interweaves our spirituality with our personality and allows us to see things from an elevated vantage point. As a result of this new self-image, we do things for different reasons and sometimes, in a different way. Our spiritual discernment is acute, and we have to learn how to navigate among people, especially those who notice our differences. God is always ahead of us in every process we go through. He prepared a clear path and made each step I took a sure step. A new personification will open us up for a new perception.

New Perception

No one can talk you out of or into a new perception. It happens as we embrace our truths through the healing process. We have to be constant in knowing where we are, in tune to our mindset, and honest about our proclivities. We also have to seek counsel or some form of accountability through a trusted friend or resource as we migrate into a new perception. Accountability is important to making life changes. It is best to work with someone who has already survived what you are coming out of or someone who is level enough to support you in your process. People who are living beside us but not *inside* of us will think they have the answers to our plights and will give their perceptions about what we should be doing or feeling and the pace it should take. Really? The role of God in our lives should only be played by Him.

No one knows us better than our Creator, the Lord. As we raise our hands, we will find ourselves invoking His presence to help us overcome ourselves. We will need Him to override our wills, take the wheel of our emotions and compass our way. This is not a rush job, but it is a paced process.

As our perception becomes new, so will the investments we make into ourselves. When I received confirmation that I would, in fact, graduate on time and become a Doctor of Philosophy, I was also processing marriage dissolution documents and DNR (do not resuscitate) documents for my father, and transitioning my oldest daughter home after her college matriculation. I decided to take *me* back and change my last name, not just on my Ph.D., but I also amended the name on my Master's degree so that my father would be honored and I would be free. I got certified to teach even more formats of aerobics and took my own personal fitness to new heights. My perception changed and my ever-changing style evolved even further: my hair styles often changed to match "the new me." My wardrobe changed to match "the new me." My connections changed to match "the new me."

I felt like I was preparing for something much bigger than me. I was thrilled to embrace a *lift* that was somehow trapped by years of barriers, blockages and bondages.

This new perception changed my life. It changed how I *saw* my life, how I managed the affairs of my life, how I looked at situations, and how I addressed circumstances. My new perception brought a freedom that literally felt like I was floating at times. I really felt my heart take flight without fear. I had new expectations and new anticipations for the outcomes of my life choices. I was now ready to take on responsible empowerment.

See then that ye walk circumspectly, not as fools, but as wise,

—*Ephesians 5:15*

Look to the Light

Your Word is a lamp for my feet, and a light on my path.

—*Psalm 119:105*

The phrase, "Look to the light," is often said to people when they are dying, but this is a phrase that should be spoken more often to encourage us while we are yet living. Once we drop our fists, we need to look to the light that is now in front of us, perhaps surrounding us. If we have come through some dark places, we are now able to see the light, so look to it, follow it, and keep moving. Not only will you see the light and feel the light, but it will also illuminate your new path. People may have always been complimenting you, and you may have missed it because it is difficult to see in the dark. When you raise your hands, you will start noticing the positive attributes of your character, your thought process, your abilities, your influence and your physique, because light brightens the image. If there are flaws, the light will pick them up, and you can decide how to address them. If there are fabulous spots, the light will pick them up, and you can choose to elaborate on them. You will glow because of the light within you that is now free to shine.

The enemy wants to keep us in the dark, hidden, silent and without relevance. When we raise our hands, we cause the enemy to go on *blackout*. We are no longer bound by silly insecurities, senseless worry and intimidating ghosts of the past. We not only have a new confidence, but we are also radiant. Our radiance is seen by others, and we have to learn to say, "Thank you!" When people compliment you, just say,

"Thank you!" When people notice something good or positive about you that you have not yet discovered about yourself, just say, "Thank you!" You may have to practice a few times before it becomes natural and unrehearsed, but you will get used to it. This was new for me. I received compliments all the time, but they affected me totally differently once I began to drop my fists and raise my hands. I did not "need" the accolades, sometimes felt a bit taken by them (and most times, felt quite undeserving), but I have learned to just say, "Thank you!" I thank God for His light in my life, and He alone is worthy of all glory. When He allows me to touch the lives of others, and they acknowledge it, I need to acknowledge *them* by simply saying, "Thank you." People are blessed when you accept their appreciation.

Look to the Light. The light is the Lord. Jesus is the light of the world. He is the light of *my* world. The more I look to His light, the more He lightens my life. The more I drop my fists and raise my hands, the more light I allow in and the more light I give.

CHAPTER BREAK

CHAPTER 5
RESPONSIBLE EMPOWERMENT

But the God of all grace, who hath called us unto His eternal glory by Christ Jesus, after that ye have suffered a while, make you perfect, establish, strengthen, settle you.

—I Peter 5:10

What is on the other side of our sufferings, disappointments, brokenness, and our dropped fists and raised hands? Empowerment. A divine power to live beyond here and move into our new now.

...The fundamental definition of empowerment means to give power to; to authorize; to enable; to permit.

Empowerment is a link, a bridge, and a conduit between pre–and post–deliverance; pre–and post–healing; and pre–and post–change. When we are truly emotionally debt free, we will experience a liberation that propels us into a new dimension; in our thought process, in our behavior, and our socialization. Change can feel uncomfortable until we adjust. For some, emotional empowerment is like opening a gate to a brand-new horizon. To others, it may feel like chains falling or even like oxygen – the ability to finally take an uninterrupted breath. It is a measurable moment that often has a significant impact and can even lead to peace of mind.

Dropping our fists and raising our hands allows God to give us the power to live autonomously from our past pain and present challenges so that we might discover new opportunities. He gives us the power to take on new possibilities, take over our fears, and to take down barriers. This is a process, and like any other process, it takes time, investment, pursuit, and patience.

While we were in bondage, we were overpowered by someone or something that dictated our life on some level or another. With divine empowerment, we have the power to influence the outcomes of our life. Of course, the divinity concept means that it is given by, fostered by, and covered by the Lord, but we are enabled to take ownership and responsibility. This includes our power to revive, reestablish and resource our life and our future.

With empowerment comes responsibility. If we do not take on this new empowerment responsibly, we can find ourselves repeating cycles.

Responsible empowerment involves taking full accountability along with taking the reins.

Let's discuss power for a minute.

It appears that society has been conditioned to associate power with possessions. People who view power in this way often fail to recognize that there is actually debt associated with this mindset. And not just financial debt, but mental and emotional debt as well. Responsible empowerment includes self-confidence, self-control, and self-contentment, respectively. A healthy concept of *self* is the foundation for empowerment. Once we have dropped our fists and raised our hands, we are free. Freedom can be intimidating at first, especially emotional freedom.

"I have the right to do anything," you say—but not everything is beneficial. "I have the right to do anything"—but not everything is constructive.

—I Corinthians 10:23 (NIV)

As we know, God has given us free will, and once we have overcome obstacles in life, we may have an entirely different outlook toward *our* will. Our *will* is powerful, for it manages our *way*. A different outlook toward our power will have an impact on the way we determine to go now that we have dropped our fists and raised our hands.

Self-Confidence

Self-confidence is not arrogance or conceit; it is feeling well, accepting well, and thinking well about *you*. It is believing in your ability, capability, skills, and experience. Feeling well indicates that you have peace, not just moments of temporary happiness, but that you have innate joy. Innate joy is not predicated by circumstance, people, places, or temporary conveniences. Innate joy is knowing that you are well. When you feel well, you can accept well. You can look at yourself through the lens of truth and be okay with the image. Self-confidence is the ability to change the images that we are not comfortable with in our own time and based upon our own choices. It is empowering to see ourselves the way God sees us. We have overcome caring about how irrelevant people perceive us, and now we accept the way we feel about ourselves without apology or explanation. This is thinking well. We now think well of who we are and what we do. If for any reason we feel that we need to make adjustments, we will make the changes—on *our* terms.

EXERCISE #4

The Shape Trade

We are going to take an audit in this exercise. We are going to walk through an old shape that is filled with "trash" (fear, unforgiveness, guilt, etc.), all the stuff that had us bound with raised fists. We are going to take an audit to separate the *trash* from the *treasure*.

You have the trash list, now, what treasures will you replace your old trash with (opportunities, trust, healthy relationships, etc)?

Notice the shapes. The "trash" is full of entrapments while the "treasure" is loaded with opportunities for expansion and growth.

Add to each list as it is applicable to you. Write down what has changed from one shape to the other. We were in bad shape, and now we are reshaped.

- What has changed in our lives from the trash to the treasure?
- How have these changes manifested in your life?

After this exercise, we can see where we are clear, determined and deliberate. We can also see where we are yet holding onto things that are meant for trash.

Self-Control

Managed passion, glory to God! Once we have raised our hands, we will be empowered to manage our emotions and to choose our passions. Empowerment gives us the authority to prioritize, to plan and to process. We are free to decide when, who, what and where. We are empowered to give the most direct response to someone or something that does not fit into our plan, "No." The first time I simply said "No," it set my new-found power in motion. Now, I give a brief explanation if challenged, and a sterner "No" if challenged beyond the boundary I have developed.

Self-control is about setting boundaries for what comes in. We must determine to not allow the trash from our past to come into our present sphere (mindset, choices, behavior, etc.). And more importantly, we must relinquish (bad habits, negative associates, dangerous proclivities, etc.).

My time was the *first* thing to be enclosed with a new boundary. I am selective and more deliberate with how I spend my time. I do not arbitrarily connect, commit, or collaborate. I have a private calendar of events, and it is as flexible as I determine it should be. I wear certain connections as a loose garment, capable of leaving it behind when necessary until I feel that they are suitable to stay. *Self-control.*

Influence also impacts self-control. Once we have established our name, our brand, or business and obtained a level of respect, we can control a lot of what happens in our sphere. Now that we have established the principle of dropping our fists and raising our hands, we have a direct and constant inner connection with the Lord like a tree planted by a river of water. We are consistently being nourished and poured into. When we get dry, we just extend ourselves to become more grounded in God's Word, in face-time, and among other like-minded people. This helps us to discern and to remain connected to what matters most. Influence is the level of empowerment that promotes peace because we are not pressured into pleasing others against our will or at our own expense. This is a new day baby!!!

"Church Service Starts at 11"

We all know that living among people is a challenge. Living with the woman in my mirror is often a chore, so just imagine all of the other people who have mirror-arguments like I do and then put them in close quarters like an office, a classroom, a supermarket, a department store, in a church or even in our homes. Mercy! Everyone has "stuff" to deal with and all together we are told to make the best effort to live at peace with them.

Although the culture in our churches is becoming more like the world in its interactions and business dealings, there are still some who are "old-school" and have an appropriate fear of the Lord and still regard how their lives bear witness to their confession of faith. In dealing with difficult people, especially those who are not Christians or church-goers, we should exercise self-control over our temperament.

Now that we have dropped our fists and raised our hands, we have to remember that we still live among difficult people who live with raised fists. We have to practice the principle in order for it to become our permanent internal point of reference *before* we respond to challenges.

One of the ways I monitor my attitude and measure my success dealing with difficult people is if I can say, "Church service starts at 11, please come join us." If I cannot invite someone to my place of worship in the midst of a challenging encounter, I may not have handled it too well.

It is important to hold ourselves accountable, realize how far we have come and to recognize where we need to yet improve. *Drop Your Fist and Raise Your Hands* is not a one-time event, it is a lifelong process.

Church service starts at 11, please come join us.

COMMERCIAL BREAK

Are we comfortable setting up new gates? A gate is an entry way into a space owned by someone, and *we* own our heart, our mind, our time, our treasure, our body, and our temperament. Are we comfortable enough with our empowerment to set up new gates or to perhaps change codes, passwords, and locks to prevent unlawful entry into our life?

Responsible empowerment requires that we review the roster of people, places, and things attached or associated with our lives. We will immediately see that we need to set up new gates to safe guard our privacy. This is necessary because new *requires* new.

Neither do people pour new wine into old wineskins.

If they do, the skins will burst; the wine will run out and the wineskins will be ruined. No, they pour new wine into new wineskins, and both are preserved.

—Matthew 9:17

We own the property and the security system surrounding our lives, so now let's protect it. Some of us are recovering from years of trying and failing to fix the broken places. Now that we have a new opportunity to safeguard ourselves, let's set up some basic parameters.

- Let's not engage solicitors selling compromise, foolery, or games.
- Let's put a code at some gates for special entry; this means that we may have to condense our core circle of friends. Everyone will not understand your change and your healing. People who understand what has transpired in your life will understand the new acronyms, colloquialisms, and idioms that may develop as you redefine your permissions.

Your investment gates will also require new passwords and locks. From this point forward we will need to carefully measure the risks to new investments we are willing to make with our heart, our time, and our money. If the liability outweighs the added value, we may have to change the password and the locks. We may revoke some keys and terminate some key holders. Change means just that. For some, it will mean that they need to find another automatic financial teller when they make foolish choices because that gate to your life has been demolished. Some people wear a sign that reads, "Love at your own risk!" Terminate their gate access. Some people are walking around in camouflage thinking no one sees them. But you do, so change the locks on the gate. Some people have become too common with you, saying cutting remarks fueled by hidden envy, but it is not hidden to you so change the password to the gate they used to enter. When they attempt to enter their code, it will not work. Their access to you will be by invitation only. In other words, do not come for me if I am not calling for you; invitation only.

If there are some business deals that have gone bad over time, set up a new gate. We have paid people for poor services long enough. Terminate their contract and establish a new gate. The intent is not to become an island or to completely cut all ties with all people, but you know who needs their access revoked, monitored, or limited—so change it.

It is time to break molds, unhealthy traditions, unrealistic expectations, and false intimacies. This will preserve your life, protect your pocket book, proclaim your peace, save your relationships, and propel your purpose. It is time to accelerate. We may have to make up for some lost time, so let's redeem the time and move forward.

Self-Contentment

Respectively, self-contentment is the final frontier to grounding ourselves in empowerment because it speaks to the balance of our essence. We are content when we are balanced spiritually, emotionally, physically, and mentally. If any one of those areas are off, it throws us off balance, and we lose power. The driving source behind our empowerment is our ability to obtain self-contentment. We are self-content when we can embrace the silence in our lives, when we can spend quality and enjoyable time alone, when we self-care, when we self-motivate and when we are creative.

There is a healthy balance between introversion and extroversion. We all need to balance between our private thoughts and our open collaborations. It is necessary to be honest about our feelings now that we have dropped our fists and raised our hands. We need to be honest about our "what now?" quandary.

It is important to do a character audit to avoid the pitfalls that may have tripped us up: swine, dogs, and foxes. Let's rid our yard of these wild beasts and enjoy being content in our newfound empowerment.

Dogs Eats Vomit and Swine Can't Catch

We have heard and may have even quoted the Biblical principle of not giving sacred things to dogs or pigs. Generally, it seems ludicrous to waste value on an animal that returns to eat its own vomit or one that rolls around in mud among other nasty things. But, practically speaking, dogs nor swine can catch.

Do not give dogs what is sacred; do not throw your pearls to pigs.

If you do, they may trample them under their feet, and turn and tear you to pieces.

—Matthew 7:6 (NIV)

Why throw something to someone who does not have the capacity or the capability to respond with a natural and plausible reaction to catch? I am finding that some concepts are not deep or mystical, but rather simple, so simple that we can miss them. This Biblical parable was expressed to prevent waste and unnecessary pain. Do not continue to offer what is valuable in you to those who have no appreciation for it. Basically, do not throw your prized possessions to someone when they are not able to catch.

Unfortunately, the reality is, most people cannot catch what you have to offer. This is a disappointing fact I know, but I have learned through trial and error that the people who can seize, hold, or make good use of my value are few. If you hide your life in God, He only reveals the true you to whom He trusts with your value.

I can no more cause a person to grip or cleave to me than I can make a dog lose its proclivity to eat vomit. It is impossible. Looking for the impossible in people is unfair to you and them because it will only frustrate you and kill them emotionally. God knows who can catch us, hold us, and seize the value that He has put in us. He will not entrust us to just anyone and certainly not anything that does not have the capability to grip. It's not *what* dogs and pigs do that disqualify them; it is their nature that limits them *indefinitely* from catching our pearls. They cannot catch by nature!

I had to identify the dog and swine encounters in my life to prevent future occurrences. There were people in my life with nasty habits behind a gentle exchange. They could not hold on to what I offered, but would repeatedly take it, mingle it with their internal filth and throw it up. Then once it was vomit (repulsive and worthless), they would eat it back up and then come back to get some more. In other words, I would offer someone the sincere essence of who I am and they would take it as if they knew what to do with it. But, they would mingle what was precious to me with something that was common, thereby taking away my value, and spit it up. Now, of course they gave me the impression that they could take care of it, understand it, and intended to treasure it, but they did not have the desire to keep it safe. They just wanted it because it appealed to them.

Do you need to identify the dogs and swine that *you* encounter?

Once you have identified these negative people in your life, distance yourself from them, release them from you, and in some cases, sever the connection. If the dog bit you, it bites. If the pig kicked mud on you, it's dirty. Learn from the experience and do not provide another opportunity for it to hurt you again.

Sobriety

Sobriety is a key component to our empowerment because it is the ability to hold ourselves together. We are empowered by how we overcome adversity, handle hot mess situations, rise above disaster, and maintain our composure during the confusion. We may not get it right 100% of the time, depending on the circumstance, but our profile should be consistent.

Now that we have adopted the principle of drop your fists and raise your hands, the enemy will try your confidence and your commitment. You got this! Just remain calm. Put your *stop screams* in a proper place, close by, so that you can easily listen to them. *Stop screams* are the internal warnings that tell us that there is danger ahead and to stop before we encounter it.

Be alert and of sober mind. Your enemy the devil prowls around like roaring lion looking for someone to devour.

—I Peter 5:8

We are given an awesome protective warning about the enemy and his antics. Our safety and our empowerment are in our sobriety. When our emotions seem to be running away, we need to pull them back in. We need to go back to the basics of fasting and praying, disciplining our inner self and bringing our essence into alignment with God's Word and God's Spirit. People want to dismiss these practices as Old Testament principles with little value, but I challenge that notion. We should take time, spend time, and commit our time to our sobriety for it to manifest in our lives. Empowerment is taking the reins of our self and steering in the right and righteous direction.

We must anchor our mindset into thinking positively, crowding out the negative innuendoes of the enemy.

Management

The process of dealing with the issues in our lives can be complicated and especially difficult to reel in once they are out of control. We can pull it together, just like any other business deal gone bad. We must plan, organize, collaborate, and strategize for the process of self-management to actualize in our lives. In short, we must take over.

Now that we have positioned ourselves in empowerment, we will take one issue at a time and lay out the plan to put them back in order. This works for financial stability, emotional stability, relationship stability and family stability. We just have to put things back into proper perspective, put our plan in place and allow God to work.

When we relinquish our tendency to control incomes and outcomes, we have power. Remember, there is no battle where there is no spoil. You are the spoil to every battle. You are of great value and speechless worth. You now have the empowerment to manage your life. You just need the right resources and the right tools. Search, seek, and pursue people and projects that are successful. Read, listen, and apply what you glean from their stories. Management is about being empowered to align our outcomes, not allowing circumstances or situations to dictate them.

EXERCISE #5

THEN AND NOW

Responsible empowerment affords us the opportunity, almost demands the obligation, to take a closing inventory of *then* and *now*. It is a good idea to look back over our lives to see the change, to measure its impact and then to canvas outcomes.

In this exercise, we will simply complete Then and Now Statements. Our "then" statement should reflect what *happened*; what intimidated, threatened and provoked us into a life with raised fists. Our "now" is post raised hands; a new mindset, a new level of courage and self-determination.

Doing this is good for several reasons. One, it allows us to see progress, two, we can speak affirmations into our own lives and finally, putting things on paper is powerful.

Let's begin. I will list a few and then you can list yours as well.

THEN	NOW
You rejected me and I felt ashamed	You decided that I was too much for you and I agree
I looked in the mirror and I was discourages	I am naked and fabulous. I will eat better, get more exercise and feel better!
I felt ignored, tolerated and diminished	I am a catalyst for change
	I have to be careful before I speak because I have great impact.

THEN	NOW
_____	_____
_____	_____
_____	_____

Remain Active

Do not stop. Now that you have a new opportunity to achieve something new, different, bigger, and out of your human capability, reach for it. Do not get distracted by the tabloids, the crowd, or the critics. Allow their stones to provide the stairs to your climb. This new momentum is fueled by your power to reach. Draw nigh unto God, asking, pressing, listening, yearning, and obeying Him.

When you are positive and muster up faith amid tragedy, you have power. When you are a peace offering in the time of someone's struggle, confusion, and hopelessness, you have power. When you are a pillar of strength by your dependence upon God's grace, you have power. When you are hated by many and respected by the same many, you have power.

Remember, you have influence; therefore, you have power. Use this power wisely. Stay active in your quest, in your craft, in your core, in your passion. Staying active simply means staying *present*. Stay in the moment. The enemy will come to distract and to dismantle you right as you are close to a break through. Cut it loose. Cut anything or anyone loose if it does not speak to your destiny. Let it fall off you like water off a duck's back. While you are climbing, you need to be weightless. Even when you are at the resting deck between climbs, remain drama-free. Do not take on another's burden to the point that you cannot climb. You can provide your ear without weighing down your heart.

Rest

Take advantage of check points. This is when you should rest. Take a moment to shut down, shut out, shut up and shut in. We all need time to re-group, re-coupe and to re-store.

It is great to incorporate a practice that helps you capture important things while you disengage like journaling, mediating, or exercising. Sleeping is, of course, the best source of rest once we have disengaged our minds from all matters. If you are married, sex is a great way to unwind. It is a biological fact that a great level of physical activity before a nice rest is good for the heart, mind, and spirit.

Empowerment is largely about balance and resting is one of its most crucial components.

Then Jesus said, "Let's go off by ourselves to a quiet place and rest awhile."

—Mark 6:31a (NLT)

It is great to spend time alone, to think or to not think, or to just sit. I love those moments when I am not required or requested. I cherish moments of "me." In these moments, we learn to appreciate ourselves. If we are single, we learn how to be okay with our singleness during check points.

After we have rested awhile, *check points* are moments we take to evaluate, to measure and to prepare. We reflect on what is working well and what we may need to adjust. This may involve our personality traits or other outside things. These are important places in empowerment because we learn a lot about ourselves. We should always be in a place of learning and growing. Even while resting we are moving forward.

REFLECTIONS

Debra R. Wilson, Ph.D.

We all should take a moment to look back over our life and think things over. What can you truly say?

I can truly say that I have been blessed and I would take nothing for my journey now. When I read back over the previous chapters in this book I cannot help but smile, laugh, shed tears and then shout. I am amazed at what I survived.

What I survived, overcame, endured and came through may not be the worst of some or the best compared to others, but it is what *God* did for me and it is so amazing!

I am on the other side of what others may have died in, became an addict in, lost their mind in or just chose to remain in, but I took the challenge to apply the principle, *Drop Your Fists and Raise Your Hands*. As a result, God caused me to triumph. I survived people who did not wish me well, I forgave my father, released toxic people from my life, restored broken relationships, and, during the most trying times in my life, I got my Ph.D.. Only God!

Obtaining my Doctorate of Philosophy, however, is not the only event that has earned me the right to be heard. My accomplishments, my failures, my lessons, my pitfalls, my triumphs, my points of anguish, my seasons of despair and my refusal to *die here* is what has brought me to this platform. This is indeed a platform; a raised place that I now stand on top of. Standing on top of what intended to bury me, bring me down, diminish me and label me. It is amazing what God can do with our lives when we surrender to Him. As we continue to drop our fists and raise our hands, we will stand on top of *it*. Whatever the *it* is in our lives, we can stand on it, use it as our stage.

To the places and the people that may have left scars, "Thank you!" When I was deemed too much, too heavy and too hard to love, "Thank you!" When you decided that you could not accept me, stick with me, help me, work with me, cover me, protect me, stand with me, receive me, or remain loyal to me, "Thank you!" For every negative word, ill thought, and sarcastic return, "Thank you!" When my encouragement was annoying, my love was overwhelming, my ministry was overbearing, and you chose to leave, "Thank you!" You have created such a stage for me and I am eternally grateful for *every* step that you donated to this platform.

Thou hast turned for me my mourning into dancing: thou has put off my sackcloth, and girded me with gladness.

—Psalms 30:11

Treasure

We can be selective about where we put our treasure now that we are empowered. We can change our investment strategies, literally and metaphorically. We can change our financial profile as well as our heart profile. We can alter our budgets and close out line items where there has been either no activity or a negative return on our past investments. The wonderful thing about empowerment is ownership. We can change as much as we need to, when we decide to and how we choose to.

We now realize that we do not have to apologize, explain, or provide notice when we cancel certain types of accounts. If the liability outweighs the asset, we need to cancel the account. If the risk outweighs the gain, we can cancel the account. If the bottom line is always red after we have put our treasure in, we should pull our treasure out.

Treasure is not just defined by money or other material investments, but it is also defined by the things we value; family, relationships, investments, wealth that we accumulate, and by sacrifices we make.

For where your treasure is, there your heart will be also.

—Matthew 6:21

Our heart drives our investments. Now that we have dropped our fists and raised our hands, we may have a change of heart, a modification to what is important, and an adjustment to what matters most. As we do an audit of our heart, we will begin to change what we treasure.

If we become deliberate in our stewardship, we will be exercising responsible empowerment. Not just in how we spend our money, save our money or make investments with our money, but also in how we manage our life, our blessings, our benefits and our advantages.

MEANINGFUL MOMENTS

The audit of our empowerment will reflect the lessons we taught to those God put in our care.

My daughters are unique individuals with one commonality, me. They seem to be like me in many ways and even have the same sometimes polarizing attributes that I possess; emotionally strong, entertaining, smart, discerning, loving, loyal and assertive. I used to worry that I would not be enough for them by myself because they are so much—so much stronger than me, have so much more potential, talent, fear, purity, joy, and life. They are exponentially more than I could dream of. My challenge is to ensure that I pour into them to the extent that I challenge them to be better all around; first to please God and then to please themselves, while serving the world. I do not want them to replicate, duplicate or mimic me, but to stand on top of what I provided and to expand their individual territories.

Responsible empowerment is not just about the differences we make in our home or our immediate spheres, but it is also about what we do beyond ourselves that can impact the world we live in and the world we will leave behind. What we do builds momentum. We are like a tree; how deep are our roots? How strong are our branches? What is the condition of our fruit? Now that we have dropped our fists and raised our hands, we have not just raised the bar, but we have also created a new bar with a new set of rules, expectations, anticipations, and dreams. We are giving God and ourselves something new to work with. We are now ready to set sail on a new adventure. What is so awesome about this is the ceiling where there is no top.

Re-direct. Dropping our fists may launch us into discovering a new means of survival. We are most likely at a cross road as we take on the challenge of adopting this principle into our lives. This may require us to take a temporary detour from "here" and re-direct our plans, our focus, our passion or our perspective. Dropping our fists is not going to be as easy as it sounds or as difficult as it appears. Re-directing may be the balance between here and there, the bridge between brokenness to victory, and the stepping stones to a new beginning.

MEANINGFUL MOMENTS
PART III

I accepted the offer of a Ph.D. Program and just kept moving forward while my life seemed to unravel around me one thread at a time. The program that I was offered did not lock me into one genre, but was broad and open enough to fulfill my creative passion to impact the lives of people. *Multidisciplinary Human Services*.

All of my life, I privately had a vision of being an impactor of change in people's lives. My Devotion to Motherhood, passion for teaching dance, love of providing counseling and mentorship, manifold ministries, and even my enthusiasm for corporate leadership, were indicative of my deep desire to impart change. I want people to perfect their purpose as I pursue and perfect mine. I want to see people reach their fullest potential and I want to be a part of the process. I get mentally claustrophobic when I am limited to one lane, one scope, one audience, and one objective. I believe this is why my life experiences were not able to take me out; I had so much that I had yet to accomplish. I would often say to the men in my life, "If you hurt me, you will not kill me," and "I refuse to die here!" They did not kill me, and I did not die. Instead, I survived, I soared, and I continued to succeed.

Fan Base

Our Fan Base should always be larger than our Fair Base. Our Fan Base are people who are enamored with our fame, who they perceive us to be, and who we allow them to see. Our Fair Base are those in our lives who tell us the truth without telling our truths to anyone else. They know you and love you for who you are. You have a reciprocal relationship with them and share some secrets. I say some, because only Jesus can handle ALL of you and your secrets. Our Fair Base knows who we are behind the scenes, when we are angry, what makes us tick, and what hurts we may be holding on to or holding back. They are part of our core life audience because they are not afraid of being brutally honest in our lives.

Buddy System

We need accountability. Our Fan Base may tell us the truth, but that does not necessarily mean they qualify as a person to hold you accountable. Bad company corrupts good manners; therefore, dropping your fists may require dropping your accomplices or at least putting a healthy distance between them.

Risk Agreements

Dropping your fists is a personal moment of truth when we face ourselves, come to ourselves and handle ourselves. What happened to us that either torments our most inner thoughts or that we have just learned to live with but never acknowledged our pain about it? What are we struggling with because we have set up house with it? A bad relationship, a bad habit, a bad feeling, a bad perception? Setting up house means that we have settled in to the degree that letting go requires some major adjustments. What have we tried and failed because "we" were in the middle of it and refused to do it God's way? What have we accepted that we know is not God's best for us? Dropping our fists requires making hard decisions about hard situations that have a hard hold on our hearts. This may require tearing up our Risk Agreements.

Ye did run well; who did hinder you that ye should not obey the truth?

—Galatians 5:7 (KJV)

Risk Agreements hinder our focus, tempt us to forfeit our life's purpose, and can even move us away from our core. We have to be careful not to take on the project of forcibly removing someone out of their own comfort zone. If they are comfortable in their condition and will not accept counsel or take heed to warnings and consequences, leave them there and allow them to work things out on their own. Do not waste time trying to convince them—against their will—of *their* potential, at your *own* expense. Such actions are often futile and can result in an unbalanced relationship and a waste of a good resource–You!

I have found who the problem is when it comes to my dilemmas, setbacks, and start-overs: me. I was taking on people like projects and forgetting that they were people just like me with the same sinew, opportunities and free will that I have.

We cannot write another person's script. We often get caught up in this micromanaging of people in our personal relationships. We want to tell another person what they should think, how they should feel and what they should have said or what they should not have said. We cannot write their script nor can they write ours. A Risk Agreement is an attempt to write or rewrite someone's script to see the movie we desire to see. When we do this, we find ourselves in compromising situations. If we put ourselves in the "driver seat" of another person's life, we have attempted to take on God's role, crippled the person from growing and extended ourselves beyond capacity. This is a form of witchcraft, trying to influence or manipulate natural order in order to distort or change natural results. So avoid risk agreements because they are traps to take us out methodically: emotionally, mentally and spiritually.

TEAR UP RISK AGREEMENTS

A Risk-Agreement is a conformity contract. It is a contract we sign internally that simply allows us to play two sides of life at the same time. The side that trusts God and the side that takes matters into our own hands. The side that praises and the side that curses. The side that is a saint on Sunday and the side that is the super-sinner by Sunday night. The side that leads people to victory and the side that lives in defeat. The side that preaches and teaches Holiness and the side that refuses to live Holy. The side that is seen doing the appropriate or politically correct thing in public and the side that privately leads a life of perversion. The side that says the right thing and the side that lives the wrong way. Do we need to continue? I think we understand.

Paul strongly urged us in Romans 12: 2 to avoid these agreements:

And be not conformed to this world: but be ye transformed by the renewing of your mind, that ye may prove what is that good, and acceptable, and perfect, will of God.

As outlined, Risk Agreements can be dangerous because they give the enemy a foothold into our lives to influence our thoughts, manipulate our emotions and to dominate our perceptions. When we attempt to "fix" things to work out our way, we have a tendency to react impulsively, totally disregard counsel or refuse to ask for advice. And yes, this too is an act of raising our fists.

A Risk Agreement is a contract that is consciously entered into. Knowing the difference between right and wrong and still refusing to do the right thing is sin. People of God have been entering into Risk-Agreements since the beginning of time. They didn't work then and will never work. The Bible is explicit about this.

For (God does not overlook sin and) the wrath of God is revealed from Heaven against all ungodliness and unrighteousness of me who in their wickedness suppress and stifle the truth, because that which is known about God is evident within them (in their inner consciousness), for God made it evident to them.

—Romans1:18-20 (AMP)

A Risk Agreement is entered into when we understand truth and what the will of God is and yet choose alternatives. This is dangerous because we have decided to take a risk with our own soul. Anytime we are not willing to listen to wisdom and respond to our own red flags; we enter into risk.

This is what makes it so difficult for a backslider or an addict to return; the mindset. Our mindset affects our heart motive and then out of the abundance of the heart, our mouth sets our actions into direction.

It is imperative that we understand the motor of the mind. It is more central to operations within us than we sometimes realize.

Let's discuss the struggle of backsliding. As soon as God delivers a backslider out of one situation, they immediately set themselves up for the next. Notice I said set themselves up? Once we begin down a risk road, it is difficult to even recognize the pattern of our actions unless or until we hit a major life road block that gets our attention. This is what is often referred to as "rock bottom."

People who are struggling with addiction are typically struggling with a decision to stop behavior that is dangerous to themselves or to those close to them. Sometimes they make the decision to stop because of some consequence that wakes them up and causes them to listen to the "stop screams." Why do Christians enter into Risk-Agreements? Because we are human and frail with a special sixth sense that we sometimes choose to ignore. The sixth sense is the Holy Spirit initiating "stop-screams" into them. So if we obviously hear these screams, why do we ignore them? Disobedience. A stubborn will. A closed heart. A double or confused mind.

The battle of our will is one of our biggest struggles. After the first Risk-Agreement was made in the garden of Eden, many generations followed the same pattern.

- The children of Israel who consistently made Risk Agreements by turning their heart against God every time He rescued them.
- Hosea's wife, Gomer, a modern time "whore," who made risk agreements by sleeping with every man for selfish gain.
- King David's premeditated adultery and murder.
- Sarah, Abraham's wife, telling her husband to have sex with her maid to manipulate God's promise.
- Lot's wife who died behind the risk agreement she made to her past that she refused to let go of.
- Peter, who tried it when he cursed the damsel for recognizing him as being a disciple of Jesus.
- Ananias and Sapphira, who didn't live to warn others when they risked truth to hold on to their earthly possessions.

These are great Biblical examples of Risk Agreements, but let's list some of the agreements that we may find ourselves in today:

- Fornication relationships
- Addictions
- Self-Hatred
- Abusive relationships
- Stagnation and loss of hunger for achievement
- Unforgiveness
- Cheating on Income Taxes
- Private perversions and proclivities

These are the typical Risk Agreements the best Christian or person with good moral judgment can fall captive to. Once we develop a habit in any of these areas, it is an Agreement. Developing a habit is to make excuses to remain attached or otherwise associated with the behavior deliberately. It means that we put the behavior before God and even before ourselves.

Now, how do we cancel these Agreements? With truth!

By the time we have negotiated the terms and conditions of the Agreement and developed a mindset to compromise, we are committed to whatever lie we have told ourselves or have accepted from someone else to sign and then execute. The only way out is to dispel the lies with truth.

It is a simple two-step process: Terminate and Walk Away.

When we add steps to this process, we are still negotiating our own terms. When we silently stay connected to the other party of the Agreement, we are still negotiating our own terms.

"How long will you waver between two opinions: If the Lord is God, follow him; but if Baal is God, follow him." But the people said nothing.

—I Kings 18:21

Jesus used many metaphorical comparisons of true worshipers vs. religious display. He was actually comparing the enemy's real threats to those who are his easy prey. Most of the time, those who are Easy Prey do not recognize their perilous position because it becomes their nomenclature. Nomenclature is a term we use to categorize, characterize or classify behaviors. People who fall into this nomenclature trap are referred to as *"Grinners."* We tend to think of hypocrites as people who parade in angel apparel but are hiding horns underneath. The label "hypocrite" like "Christian," is becoming a broad term. The "roles" of the people in the church are sometimes hard to separate from the "behaviors" of the people who fill these roles. This is the characteristic of the *Grinner.*

Beware of Grinners

Grinners are also referred to as Hypocrites. Grinners are those who spend most of their time manipulating behind a smile. A seasoned person can appreciate this term. Many of us were not spared the rod for "grinnin'." When our parents were impending judgment on our behavior, the worst thing we could have done was "grin." This ridiculous response was deemed disrespectful because it was an attitude of loftiness.

You will often find Grinners scoffing, jeering, sneering, snickering or being, what my mom called, "Flippant." Flippancy is another term for a haughty spirit. For this reason, Grinners are easy prey for the enemy. They are easy prey because their behavior becomes their profile; it is habitual and predictable.

The alarming situation we face, as Jesus did, is that many Grinners are leaders in the church, in Congress, and in the corporate world. It is one thing when the enemy sews tares among the wheat of believers, but it's a totally different issue when he sews tares among leaders. This is a major cause for so much division in the nation.

Many grinners have allowed their conscious to be seared and their heart to become cold as wax. They have also become manipulators, mutilators, liars, cheaters, and haters. Grinners are often unforgiving, boisterous, rude, slanderous and double-minded.

Today, we often misdiagnose this behavior as bi-polar or some other mental illness and medicate people inappropriately. Instability in a person's life can be a result of them being double-minded. It may resemble a mental condition because their rationality is skewed, but some of the behaviors we seek to medicate is actually the condition of a hard heart.

A double minded man is unstable in all his ways.

—James 1:8

The danger of this condition is that people refuse to repent and choose to operate in this state of disillusion. They have justified their behavior for so long, they can preach against it, set policy against it, and claim to despise it while at the same time manage to comfortably live in it.

They are so deceived that they can see their behavior in others, but not in their own mirror. As a result, they do not see the need for change.

Grinners often believe they are righteous because they are in the spot light for doing good deeds. The greatest opposition that Jesus dealt with in his earthly ministry were the *Grinners*: the readers of the Law, the teachers of the Law, and the High Priests—the Church. Those who claim to know the Way and instead just stand in the way, get in the way, pervert the way and need to get out of the way.

Unbelievers are already mobilized for the enemy, many times unaware, but *Grinners* actually enlist.

Grinners know the way, but choose to enter a Risk-Agreement with the enemy to their own eventual demise. Grinners scoff, snicker and find fault with everybody and oppose every idea that's not their own or those they do not understand. A lot of tainted innocence is attributed to the hands of the Grinner because they discourage and destroy others.

Grinners are false teachers, false prophets and depict the position of the antichrist today. That may sound strong and over the top, but the definition of "antichrist" that Paul gave is anyone who does not proclaim Jesus to be the Christ. I believe this extends beyond what a person says and also includes motives and actions. This is a continuing battle within our society today. The battle did not begin with this generation, but it has definitely worsened over time.

How do *Grinners* stop the madness? The same way we all do. Drop their fists and raise their hands. We do not have to live in bondage.

Irrational thinking is bondage. Rejecting truth is bondage. Living in risk, at risk, and with a risk, is bondage.

I decree and declare that from the day you read this book, if not just this section, that you shall drop your fists. I declare that you are no longer a victim because God has paid the price for your healing and with His stripes you are healed. You have the victory. Now, let's "Drop em!"

Drop your fists!

Principles of Empowerment

There are three principles to Responsible Empowerment that will provide strength, self-control and serenity: Divine Order, No Harm and No Foul. Together, these three principles provide liberty from revisiting the sting of a painful experience or event and helps to prepare our hearts for revisiting the place or the people who may have left scars on our lives in some way. The principles provide preparation because there is a strong possibility that we will have the opportunity to overcome the imageries that may have lingered past our deliverance and healing experience while taking this journey (because our minds are created to remember such). In addition, we may be blessed with the opportunity to pour into or otherwise bless someone who is wounded and waiting for forgiveness, acceptance, deliverance or emotional healing just like we may have been. We may encounter people who intended to harm us in some way, or who attempted to harm us, or yes, who actually *did* harm us in some way. We may also encounter someone who we may have harmed, intended to harm or desired to harm in some way as well. Regardless of the circumstances, it will be an opportunity to live in the principle of Drop Your Fists and Raise Your Hands.

1. <u>Divine Order</u>

If we trust in the Lord and in the power of His might and believe in His sovereignty and His wisdom, we learn to trust His timing. God has divine order in our lives and He is supreme at bringing *things* into order at the right time; although, His timing may challenge our "readiness.

We opened our discussion with a story about Joseph and his brothers. We understand that Joseph had to endure several painful experiences at the hands of his brothers, but we also understand that this hurt did not just touch Joseph's life. It burdened the life of his father and even his brothers who sold him off. His brothers acted irrationally, foolishly and with contempt against Joseph because of their jealousy, pride, arrogance, fear, anger, and sense of entitlement. Years later, the threat that lit the fuse for their fury would come around again, but this time, the reality would produce fear, shame, guilt and speechless amazement. Joseph's family was experiencing the worst famine in their land, to the point of devastation and impending death. Their circumstance would lead his ten brothers to buy corn in Egypt where of course, Joseph was now the governor over all the land. Joseph was the primary distributor who sold food to all the people of the land, so when his brothers came, it was Joseph who they bowed in front of with all humility to buy corn. Divine order.

There is a plethora of scriptures about the fate of our enemies and how God will deal with them on His terms and in His time. We do not benefit from these promises when we raise our fists and attempt to handle them ourselves. When we are saved, we are called to peace, even in battle.

In God's divine order, we may actually see the plight of our enemy and just when we might remember all of the quotes about God's wrath upon them, God will send a scripture *our* way to put us in check.

Do not gloat when your enemy falls; when they stumble, do not let your heart rejoice.

—*Proverbs 24:17*

Wow really? Yes, indeed. God will not allow us to act against His divine will even when we may believe we are justified to do so. It is as if God dispatches His army of angels to bridle our tongue while He works on our hearts. His love transcends us being right and them being wrong.

God's divine order dictates the rules of engagement should there be an opportunity to revisit the places and the people that left scars in our lives. The world's system refers to these divine events as karma, based upon Buddhism influence.

The idea of Karma is limited because it falls short of grace, forgiveness and mercy. Jesus fulfills the divine order by demanding that love be shown to our enemies; blessings and not cursings, peace and not revenge, love and not hate.

2. <u>No Harm</u>

Joseph recognized his older brothers when they presented themselves before him and bowed in his presence. He remembered his dream. Joseph played games with his brothers, but he did not hurt them with his empowerment. He blessed them beyond their expectations.

God will put us into a position of empowerment, but He requires obedience. We are required to obey His Word and His Spirit. We should trust God and what he puts in us regardless of our feelings, fears, concerns, etc. Dropping our fists will become a natural response as we are put into situations that will require use of the principle. The process might seem odd at first, especially when we are challenged to act against our feelings. Once we master the process, God will be able to trust us enough to put us in positions of power.

God will humble the proud and leave them speechless.

"....And his brethren could not answer him; for they were troubled at his presence."

—Genesis 45:3

God will cause people who deliberately hurt you to become subjected to you, to have to face you on the other side of your broken place and to need you. You may find a horrible ex-boss in front of you, interviewing for a position at a company you manage or even own. You might be asked to testify on behalf of someone who intended to destroy your reputation. The individual who rejected your kindness may need you to show kindness to bail them out of a situation. Your child, who may have cursed you to your face, will need you when their child hurts them in a worse way. Your parent or spouse who may have abused you may need you to provide for them in some way. The person who abandoned you may come to you for forgiveness. In all of these potential circumstances, responsible empowerment means that we *do no harm*. It does not mean that we lay up with the rapist, open a joint account with the embezzler or shack up with the abuser. It does mean, however, that we remember the promises of God upon our lives and that we act accordingly and show kindness, from our heart, with our actions and in our conduct. *No harm*.

When we raise our hands to God, we are surrendering our entire selves to Him and allowing Him to flow freely through us. There are times when this may feel like an out-of-body experience, and it is. God will supernaturally provide us with strength to genuinely forgive. Only God can heal on this deep level and bring us to a place of closure where the hurt and the pain no longer stings or is not even remembered. When God healed my heart toward my father, I no longer saw him the way I did for many years. During the conservatorship battle because of his progressive dementia, he said ruthless things to me and even his temporary female friend referred to me as an orphan. My God! Excuse the pause. I had to clap my hands on that one. While this female friend was given temporary conservatorship over my father's health, he ended up on his living room floor, face down, with more than third degree burns on his legs (and the bandages on his legs had not been changed for several weeks). I was called in for an emergency intervention. God supernaturally caused me to responsibly allow the authorities to deal with the temporary female friend while I took dad out of harm's way and became empowered with full conservatorship. *No harm*.

3. <u>No Foul</u>

Responsible empowerment means that we will operate in a spirit of fairness without undercutting, slighting, cheating or acting contrary to what is right. We will give people what we owe them even if they may have stolen from us. We will honor our vows to someone even while or if they are unfaithful to the vow they may have made to us or with us. We will remain faithful in the midst of a corrupt situation. We are responsible for how we live and not for the way others live. That is God's business. Of course, we know this, and may even say it, but when we have an opportunity to shave off just a little "get em," God is still ever present.

After Joseph tried the heart of his brothers, revealed his identity to them and talked them through forgiveness, he sent them back to get his father and took *extra* care of them. The no foul principle is an easier pill to swallow when it is God responding to *our* malicious, malign or just ignorant behavior. But how do we treat others on the other side of our broken place, once we are delivered, healed and set free? How do we entreat people that have not overcome their personal struggles, proclivities or issues yet? How do we judge them in our hearts? *No foul*.

Do we have people on our payroll that we undercut in our hearts? Are we living *among* them and then speaking *about* them to others? Are we careful in *how* we say things to other people and not just what we say to them? Are we attempting to travel outside of the grace, mercy and love boundary of ministry and teaching something beyond repent, for the day of the Lord is at hand? Are we consulting God before we canvas another person's life to ensure that we are speaking a Word in season and not just counter transferring our unresolved issues, opinions and preferences? *No foul*. Do we judge people for the same behavior, attitudes, and conduct that we mirror? *No foul*.

Joseph understood the dream that God gave him as a boy once his brothers stood before him and he was now empowered to make a difference. Joseph allowed his pain to process him into responsible empowerment. Have we allowed our past and present pains, hurts, and broken places to process us into responsible empowerment? Dropping our fists and raising our hands is a principle that enables us to do just that. Through applying the principle, we allow God to show us the truth and we face it. We allow God to present us with facts and we address them. We allow God to go into the deeply hidden parts of who we are and touch the real root of our pain and we raise our hands to Him and surrender.

When I took over my father's life through conservatorship, my goal was to keep him as comfortable in his own home as long as possible. I considered taking a leave of absence from work, but my daughters convinced me that was not the solution. I hired people to take care of him while I closely monitored and documented medication dispensing, bathing times, feeding times, etc. Dad was just becoming too weak and was not able to communicate when people were not treating him right. It was a hard place for me and my daughters. One caregiver gave my father alcohol before leaving him over night. My father laid in his own feces over night when he attempted to go to the bathroom and fell without the ability to get back up. The next morning, I received a call from the caregiver who was not able to get my father to open the door. We had to call the paramedics to get inside. I dismissed the caregiver and, with the help of a friend, cleaned up my father and the mess. I paid the caregiver for his time served, up to and including the incident. My family did not approve, but I felt it was fair. It was also fair that he received final payment on his final date of employment. And of course, the caregiver did not agree with my decision to terminate him, but I felt it was *more* than fair. *No foul.*

Responsible empowerment requires that we use the best judgment possible, especially in business affairs. We have to be deliberate in our business exchanges. It may provide a safeguard when handling personal issues as well. I have learned to close malignant personal issues as a business deal gone bad in order to pull my emotions out of the situation and make a good decision. An apology does not automatically indicate reconciliation. Some people are masters at apologizing because they are constantly offending. Apologizing is almost an art for them because aggrieving people has become their normal pattern of behavior. The abuser knows how to knock you out, put salve on the bruise and bring flowers the next day. Responsible empowerment will raise a standard. The standard becomes the new rule and the exclamation point at the end of the sentence. "No" will mean "no" and "yes" will mean "yes." Let me think about it will be respected and not today will be accepted. When people attempt to walk into my personal space with nonsense, I simply tell them, "Not today!" *No foul*. Responsible empowerment can shut down a situation before it becomes foul.

The time is always right to do what is right.

—Martin Luther King, Jr.

"Yet!"

This is God's conclusion of the book, His message to us; to you who chose to take this journey and to me who obeyed to document it.

I closed the book after my final meaningful moments because it *felt* like a good ending, it seemed reasonable to put a period there, and *I* was finished. But I heard the Lord say that I need to discuss "Yet" phrases and provide us with a hunger to stir up a yearning for *more*. More shall come by Him and through Him now that we have chosen Him in *all* matters to handle things pertaining to our lives.

Dropping our fists and raising our hands is a two-part principle that intends to draw us out of whatever prevented us (dropping) and bring us to what God has for us on the other side (raising). We are repositioned in battle. Even more so, we are empowered with tools for victory-living. We now have concepts for perceiving, changing, managing, standing, fighting, and for surrendering. It is time to change our vernacular. It is time to change our hearts.

There are some things we were expecting to change in this transformation process within, and as we took this journey, we began to feel better about them, but we do not see the manifestation "yet."

There are some dreams, aspirations and inspirations that we have not accomplished "yet." We may have pushed them aside while dealing with issues. Now that we have dropped our fists and raised our hands, we should expect these desires to come into view again.

Thank you for taking this journey with me.

Now, let's change the way we speak of our future, and let us also change our expectations and our anticipations. We will use powerful "yet" phrases to get back up, pull it together, reframe and prepare for what is next.

I will start the list and give you space to complete it.

I gotta "YET" phrase!

I have not started my business *yet*.

I have not put in for my retirement *yet*.

I have not written my screenplay *yet*.

I have not chosen the new color scheme for my new office building *yet*.

_____...yet.

_____...yet.

_____...yet.

_____...yet.

_____...yet.

Eye hath not seen, nor ear heard, neither have entered into the heart of man, the things which God hath prepared for them that love Him.

—I Corinthians 2:9

CHAPTER BREAK

BOOK CLUB
DISCUSSION GUIDE

Book Clubs are fun and offer a wealth of opportunity to personally reflect, hear the opinions of others and collaborate to determine areas of commonality. This book offers many dynamics that can benefit a study group from various viewpoints.

It is important to consider the group dynamics, such as participants, culture, sensitivity and other elements that can make the sharing experiences safe, constructive, edifying and beneficial.

A few suggestions are offered to help get started. Remember, *Drop Your Fists and Raise Your Hands* is intended to help people heal and experience peace as they journey beyond "here." Taking this journey with a group can make the experience even easier and less intimidating.

Also, there is a *Drop Your Fists and Raise Your Hands* 30-Day Journal that complements the book. Book Clubs will especially benefit from using the journal with the book by holding each other accountable for journal entries, sharing their thoughts captured in the journal, and by setting individual and, perhaps collaborative goals. Documenting objectives and setting measurable goals that have deadlines are effective catalysts for change.

Group Size and Dynamics

Determining your Book Club size for *Drop Your Fists and Raise Your Hands* will be unique because of the various and variable subject matters discussed in this book. There are some general concepts in the book that will be safe to discuss in most group dynamics; however, there are more personal and sensitive issues that may require a more deliberate approach with selective, smaller groups. To this end, one may consider further delineation by age, gender, and position or role. It is important to keep the discussion environment safe and inclusive. The proposed questions for the Book Club may help determine the best approach for your group.

Facilitation

It is always a good idea to have a discussion lead by facilitation, either by the same person or by allowing members to alternate (depending upon how the discussion will take place). The Facilitator should lead the discussion by proposing questions as suggested within this guide or by assigning other questions before the group meeting. This gives participants time to read, meditate and think about their feelings before they share their thoughts openly with the group.

Discussion Options

This book addresses past hurts, present pains and perceived threats for participants to discover and explore for the purpose of confronting personal issues, communication, and closure. For each discussion question, participants should address the following:

1. Concepts to Ponder
2. Questions to Answer
3. Feelings to Explore
4. Empowerment in Motion

Each discussion point should challenge the participant to introspectively acknowledge, understand and address their heart's response to the areas that may still need closure. For example, Dr. Wilson shares her feelings about her father before his abuse started in the home, once it progressed and once it was over. As a discussion point, the group may discuss abuse. A template to address such topics is outlined below. The template includes a discussion point and the concepts to help with introspection and open share.

Discussion point: Address *Abuse*, the number one destroyer of the home. Group participants will do the following:

1) Concepts to Ponder:
   a) Define the term *Abuse*
   b) Discuss Various Dimensions of *Abuse*
   c) Identify practical examples of *Abuse*

2) Questions to Answer:
   a) Have you ever experienced *abuse* as you have either defined or identified?
   b) Are you currently in an abusive situation in your relationship, at home, at school, at work, or at church?
   c) If so, have you determined to get out of it?
   d) If not directly, have you witnessed someone in an abusive situation?

3) Feelings to explore:
   a) Discuss how you feel and felt about the experience
   b) Discuss when you will know or knew it was time to get out
   c) Discuss how the experience affected your time, your talents, your treasures and your temperament

4) Empowerment in Motion
   a) What does empowerment look like in your life now that you have taken the challenge

to apply the principle of *Drop Your Fists and Raise Your Hands*?

b) Do you feel that you now have empowerment over your past issues that caused raised fists?

Exercise Review

- There are several exercises in this book. These are presented to allow readers to become active participants in their own change. The exercises are thought and heart provoking to help readers apply what they are gleaning from the book and to write down how these enlightenments impact their lives.

- The journal is a great place to revisit some of the exercises. Consider the options outlined below. These options work great in group settings to facilitate open sharing and principle application.

- The participants may decide to share how they addressed a particular exercise in the book. This may spawn open discussion points that the facilitator can use to expand the conversation.

Personal Reflections and Meaningful Moments

This may be a bit more sensitive as it involves personal areas that individuals may not feel comfortable sharing openly. This is where the journal becomes a great companion when reading and reflecting. Participants can privately express their thoughts and then choose which points they feel comfortable sharing.

The group may decide to address Dr. Wilson's reflections or meaningful moments in such a way that is non-invasive for group sharing. For example, Dr. Wilson discloses different relationships she experienced, encountered or endured. The discussion can explore the why, the when, the how, and the what of *Dr. Wilson's* disclosures as a way of fostering change in behaviors, perceptions or perspectives. Some options are presented below.

- The group may decide to take each experience and determine the lessons learned. For example:
  - After I left the abusive relationship, I learned how to avoid unhealthy behaviors that lead to bad choices such as,.....
  - I stopped becoming the Bail Bond for my family by not allowing myself to be pulled into the solution, but just providing support.

- The group may decide to role play from the various stories Dr. Wilson shared and discover other possible outcomes.
  - Have you ever experienced any of the relationship types described by

Dr. Wilson? a) My Escape, b) My Salve or c) Blind Spot
- o What are your thoughts about the Principles of Empowerment described in Chapter V? 1) Divine Order, 2) No Harm, and 3) No Foul.
  - o
- The group may decide to simply share how they relate to one or more the characters.

Bible Study

There are plenty of Biblical references to supply a Bible Study. The group may decide to expound on a topic, discovering more cross references to open more dialogue.

The Bible Study could focus on several areas:
- Character Study:
  - o Discuss a time, like Joseph, when you felt betrayed.
  - o Discuss a time, like David, where you felt like an outcast.
- Topical Study:
  - o What does it mean to "overcome"?
  - o The book suggests that healing follows deliverance. What are your thoughts about this process?
  - o Have you discovered any Blind Spots in your life? Have you exposed, addressed and gotten rid of them?

- Personal Life Application Study:
  - What continuing battle have you discovered after reading the book?
  - Now that you understand the "hit list," describe how you feel about temporary setbacks.
  - Are you in the Drop Your Fists or the Raise Your Hands part of the principle?
- Marriage and Family:
  - Discuss a dynamic in your personal relationships that mirror those described in the book: abuse, unfaithfulness, intimacy, etc.
  - Have you identified any *tares* growing among the wheat in your home?
- Emotions:
  - Describe the emotions you feel that may have caused raised fists in your life.
  - Describe an event or experience in your life that felt like an "emotional drive-by."
  - Have you applied the principle Drop Your Fists and Raise Your Hands to deal with any lingering feelings you may have had, like depression, bitterness, resentment, guilt, fear, anger, etc.?

ABOUT THE AUTHOR

Dr. Debra R. Wilson has been an active conference speaker and instructor for more than 25 years. She is a Certified Professional Organization and Life Coach, and the Founder of Perfecting-Purpose.com.

Perfecting-Purpose.com collaborates with clients in a thought-provoking and creative process that inspires them to maximize their personal and professional potential.

Dr. Wilson is a Consultant, Curriculum Developer, Teacher, Author, and Minister. She has been providing professional and personal life coaching as well as leadership development in several venues for over a decade.

Dr. Wilson has a Bachelor of Science Degree in Health Science—Health Care Organization and Management, a Master of Science Degree in Counseling Studies, completed graduate courses in Exegetical Theology, and she is a Doctor of Philosophy in Multidisciplinary Human Services.

Debra is the proud mother of two daughters. She is a Certified Group Exercise Instructor and has worked in the public sector for 20 years. She is a Change Manager and a Deputized Purchasing Agent where she manages the County Administrative Office Contracts/Purchasing

Division. Dr. Wilson provides contract management, project management; writes, creates, and implements training curriculum, as well as provides instruction and professional development across 27 County Departments and Agencies.

ACKNOWLEDGEMENTS

First and above all, I thank God for His love, patience, anointing, deliverance and healing. It is in Him that I live, move and have my being.

- *Cynthia, my Hero. You are an inspirational sister and friend. Thank you for your constant love and support.*
- *Ebby. Thank you for beginning the proofing process of this work for me. Thank you more so, for your friendship and support.*
- *Jennifer, Mary, Angela, Harriet and Marlene. My longtime friends and sisters. Thank you for your inspiration and manifold deposits that brought this work to the forefront.*
- *Quita, thank you for your encouragement and support. Thank you for allowing me to bend your ear and to squeeze your hand as I birthed this work.*
- *Matt, my brother and friend. Thank you for your love, support and anticipation that continues to propel me to accomplish greatness.*
- *Tasha, my God daughter, thank you. Thank you for your support and for your belief in my capacity when I became anxious along the way.*
- *Shunda, my sister. Thank you for always encouraging me to "Lift Him UP" in all things. Thank you expecting me to finish this work!*

- *Valencia, thank you for believing me and for believing in me. Thank you for helping me to stay the course.*
- *Victoria, mi Hermana in Cristo siempre. Thank you for being an active participant in my life-process. Thank you for sharing your life with me.*
- *HOPM Church Family. Thank you for your love, intercession, impartations and unity.*
- *Family and Friends who support this endeavor; thank you. Your love lifts me.*

A special, "Thank You" to all who will read and participate in the journey of this book. It is God's great pleasure to use this work to bless you, to heal your heart and to motivate you to seize new opportunities in pursuit of greatness.

To the people I admire:

KLM. Thank you your love, friendship and resolve to be "present" beyond this book.

Bishop Theodore Dexter Jakes. You have been an inspiration and compelling force behind my deliverance, healing and motivation to continue. Thank you for impacting the world by capitalizing on your never-ending season.

Kalah and Autumn. Your strength, protection, wholesomeness and authenticity centers my world. You are more than I could have imagined my life to hold.

A WORD FROM THE AUTHOR

I prayed for you. I prayed that you would take this journey with me toward your personal healing and empowerment. I prayed that every one and every thing that sought to discourage, dismantle and take you out be cast out of your life and that you will now walk in your new personification.

I hope you enjoyed *Drop Your Fists and Raise Your Hands*. It was an arduous project, but well worth it if it helped you. I would like to hear your thoughts! Please leave a review on Amazon, Goodreads, and other review sites.

You can friend me on Facebook.

http://www.facebook.com/perfectingpurpose

You can also contact me via my website or email:

http://perfectingpurpose.com

Perfectingpurpose15@gmail.com

Expect the Great!

Dr Wilson

REFERENCES FOR REFORMATION

I am finding it hard to forgive
Exodus 14:14
Matthew 18:21,22
Psalm 103:10

I need to walk away, but it is hard
Proverbs 22:24-25
Matthew 5:30
I Corinthians 10:13

I am depressed
Deuteronomy 31:8
Psalm 34:17
Psalm 40:1-3

I am losing this battle
Deuteronomy 20:4
John 16:33
Ephesians 6:13

How do I start over?
Isaiah 43:18-19
Jeremiah 29:11
Romans 8:38

I can't stop crying, it really hurts
Revelation 21:4
Psalm 138:8
Jeremiah 31:16

I am afraid
Isaiah 41:10
2 Timothy 1:7
Philippians 4:6

I need God to get me out of "here"
Psalm 34:19
Nahum 1:7
2 Corinthians 4:8-9

I feel like this will never end
Psalm 37:10-11
I Corinthians 2:9
I Peter 5:7

I am losing hope
Isaiah 54: 2-3
Psalm 3:2-6
Luke 18:35-43

How do I overcome rejection?
I Peter 2:4
Psalm 27:10
Romans 8:31

I do not feel safe
Psalm 91:7
Psalm 32:7
Exodus 14:14

I am overwhelmed
Isaiah 54:17
Psalm 16:1
Philippians 4:13

How do I forgive myself
Philippians 4:8
Psalm 103:11
Romans 8:1

I can't feel God
Exodus 33:14
Psalm 16:11
Matthew 18:20

How do I remain empowered?
Isaiah 40:29-31
Psalm 22:19
Habakkuk 3:19

Made in the USA
San Bernardino, CA
06 May 2017